THE METRICS OF
HUMAN
CONSCIOUSNESS

RICHARD BARRETT

ISBN: 978-1-291-98796-6 (sc)
ISBN: 978-1-4834-2345-6 (e)

Because of the dynamic nature of the Internet, any web addresses or links contained in
this book may have changed since publication and may no longer be valid. The views
expressed in this work are solely those of the author and do not necessarily reflect the
views of the publisher, and the publisher hereby disclaims any responsibility for them.

Any people depicted in stock imagery provided by Thinkstock are models,
and such images are being used for illustrative purposes only.
Certain stock imagery © Thinkstock.

Lulu Publishing Services rev. date: 01/02/2014

CONTENTS

FIGURES AND TABLES

Figures

Tables

The information contained in this book is drawn from my most recent publications: *Evolutionary Coaching (2014)*, *The Values-Driven Organization (2013)*, *What My Soul Told Me (2012)*, *Love, Fear and the Destiny of Nations (2011)* and *The New Leadership Paradigm (2010)*.

"Every noble work is at first impossible." – Thomas Carlyle

FOREWORD

The genesis of this book dates back to the time when Richard met Marc at a conference on Conscious Capitalism, held at the Esalen Institute in Big Sur, California in 2012. Richard was at the conference to present a paper on measuring the consciousness of leaders and organizations. Marc was at the conference to present a paper on the concept of the Unique Self. Very quickly, the conversation between the two of them turned to developing a metric for measuring the consciousness of the Unique Self.[1]

After the conference Marc broadened the conversation with Richard to involve Zak Stein, the Academic Director of the Center for Integral Wisdom, and Ken Wilber, one of the co-founders of the Center. After several conversations, we (Marc and Zak) asked Richard to begin to explore the possibility of constructing a Unique Self metric. Richard accepted the challenge and joined the board of the Center as senior scholar. This book represents the first output of this exercise.

From the beginning, the nature of the task raised some important questions. How can something as intangible as the Unique Self, which is a structure of consciousness, be measured? The popular fallacy is that measurement relates only to the objective, tangible world of the physical sciences, not to the subjective, intangible world of consciousness. So why were we and the Center keen to pursue this line of inquiry?

We believe history has shown us that the evolution of measurement is fundamental to the evolution of societies. Today, we take for granted the standardized systems of physical measurement in our daily lives, in the advancement of science, the functioning of industry and the management of the broader economy.

When you go to the grocery store, you don't give a second thought to the accuracy or reliability of the marked weight or volume of the goods that you buy. But next time you buy meat for your family or fuel for your car, notice that there is a government-backed certification of accuracy on the scale or pump. This certification assures you that the pound of meat you purchase is truly a pound and the gallon of fuel you buy is truly a gallon.

These systems of measurement, which we now take for granted, took centuries to evolve and their widespread use involved a series of political revolutions, particularly regarding the institutionalization of the concepts of justice and equality. As one of the rallying cries for the French Revolution put it, "one measure for all humanity for all time".

Because of the long history of the abuse of measures (and the abuse of people through the misuse of measures), the standardization and legal institutionalization of objective measurement was understood to be a social justice issue and an essential component of democratic governance. It is not a coincidence that the universal figure of justice holds a set of scales in one hand to represent impartiality, and a sword in the other to symbolize power. The impartiality is emphasized by the blindfold that she is wearing.

The profound importance of establishing a just measuring system is illustrated by the fact that several of the first Presidents of the United States mentioned the standardization of weights and measures in their State of the Union Addresses.

Once established, issues concerning measurement did not reappear in presidential discourse for nearly two centuries. Only in the 1970s did most post-industrial societies become concerned with standardized educational testing; so called "human capital metrics" came to be considered just as essential to the progress of the nation and the economy in the twentieth century as physical measures of weight and volume were in the eighteenth century.

So today, with measures of our scientific, economic and educational worlds firmly established, we are being challenged to seek out ways of measuring our psychological and social world. Consciousness has become the new "raw material" of the knowledge economy.

Just as physical measurement became a social justice issue centuries ago, consciousness is becoming a social justice issue now, hence the growing importance of movements such as conscious capitalism, environmental sustainability and the increasing popular resistance to undemocratic regimes.

As Einstein indicated, we cannot solve the problems we have created with the same level of consciousness that we created them. This is why we need to define more clearly what levels of consciousness we are operating from and what levels of consciousness we need to move to in order to resolve the current issues our global society is facing.

What is true for the knowledge economy has also become true in the field of education.[2] From the increasing use of standardized tests at all levels of schooling, to the widespread use of the Myers-Briggs test and others like it in business and industry, the proliferation of psychological measurement systems has been exponential in recent decades.

The modern catchphrase in industry, science, and increasingly in education is "if it can't be measured, then it doesn't exist". This is why we need to support and pursue radical innovations in the development of psychological measurement technologies, because our ability to measure something changes the conversation not just about what exists, but what we should invest in and what we should cherish in our global society.

Of course, there are some who believe consciousness cannot be measured, that the mind is too intangible or too complex to be amenable to measurement. On the one hand this is true; some aspects of the mind will always escape objectification. On the other hand, as theorists and researchers such as Habermas and Wilber have shown, there are ways to measure psychological qualities and properties, and there are ways to turn subjects into objects. In this context, we simply cannot have too much debate about what psychological or consciousness traits matter, which of them are worth measuring and how these measures should be used to improve the functioning of our society.

This leads us to the value of the pioneering work you have before you. Richard Barrett offers us an exciting new direction for measuring consciousness. He has proven that the insights these measures bring can significantly improve our individual, organizational and societal performance. While much work remains to be done in refining and operationalizing what is offered in these pages to the task of measuring the Unique Self, the work of the Barrett Values Centre stands as a testament to what can be achieved by seriously applying ourselves to the measurement of conscious.

Dr. Marc Gafni, Co-Founder and Director,
Center for Integral Wisdom
Dr. Zachary Stein, Academic Director,
Center for Integral Wisdom
October 2014

Notes

1. Marc Gafni, *Your Unique Self: The Radical Path to Personal Enlightenment* (Integral Publishers: Tucson), 2012.
2. Zachary Stein, *Tipping the scales: Social Justice and Educational Measurement.* (Doctoral Dissertation) (Harvard University Graduate School of Education. Cambridge, MA), 2014.

1

Background

I started work on defining the metrics of human consciousness around 1995. It was an accident really; I was trying to bring together the ideas of Vedic philosophy regarding the higher levels of consciousness and Maslow's hierarchy of needs. It struck me that the different graduations of higher levels of consciousness, as expressed in the Vedic tradition, corresponded to the varying degrees of self-actualization expressed by Maslow. From this research came the idea for the Seven Levels of Consciousness Model (an overview of the origins of this model can be found in Annex 1).

Once I had defined the model, I quickly realized that specific values and behaviours could be associated with each level of consciousness, and consequently, if you could ascertain the values of an individual or group you could identify what levels of consciousness they were operating from. The measuring system I developed became known as the Cultural Transformation Tools (CTT). In 1997, I formed a company, the Barrett Values Centre (BVC), and began to use the measuring system to map the consciousness of leaders and organizations.[1]

Over the years, based on feedback from users of the CTT, we made some adjustments to the measuring system, improving its reliability and validity. Now, more than sixteen years later, we have a well-established and globally-recognized set of tools for mapping the values and measuring the consciousness of individuals and human group structures (teams, organizations, communities and nations). To date

(Winter 2014), BVC has used the tools to measure the consciousness of more than 5,000 organizations, 4,000 leaders and 24 nations.

In recent years, I began to recognize that in addition to mapping human consciousness, the Seven Levels Model could also be used as a template to describe the stages of human psychological development. Figure 1.1 shows the stages of psychological development and their correspondence with the seven levels of consciousness. We grow in stages (of psychological development) and we operate at levels (of consciousness).

Figure 1.1: Stages of psychological development
and levels of consciousness.

Stages	Levels	
Serving	Service	(7)
Integrating	Making a difference	(6)
Self-actualizing	Internal cohesion	(5)
Individuating	Transformation	(4)
Differentiating	Self-esteem	(3)
Conforming	Relationship	(2)
Surviving	Survival	(1)

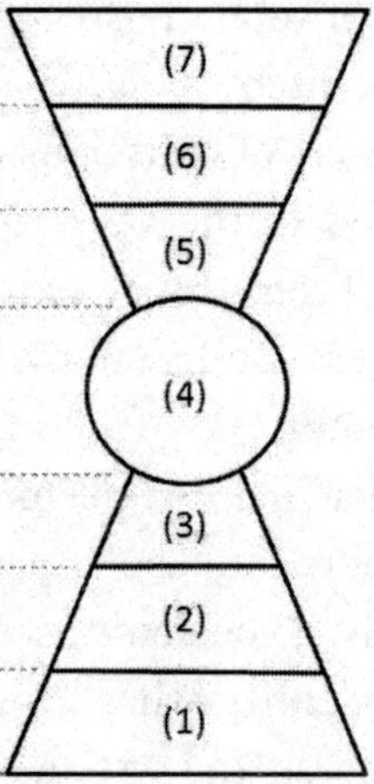

Under normal circumstances, the level of consciousness you are operating from will be the same as the stage of psychological development you have reached. However, no matter what stage of psychological development you are at, when you are faced with what you consider to be a potentially negative change in your circumstances or a situation that you believe could threaten your internal stability or external equilibrium—anything that brings up fear—you may temporarily shift to one of the three lower levels of consciousness.

Alternatively, if you have a "peak" experience—an experience of euphoria, harmony or connectedness of a mystical or spiritual nature— you may temporarily "jump" to a higher level of consciousness.

When the threat or peak experience has passed, you will return to the level of consciousness that corresponds to the stage of psychological development you were at before the experience occurred. In rare situations, a peak experience may have a lasting impact, causing you to shift to a higher stage of psychological development and operate from a higher level of consciousness.

Similarly a "negative" experience, if it is traumatic enough, and particularly if it occurs in your childhood and teenage years, can impede your future psychological development by causing you to be anchored, through frequent triggering of the traumatic memory, into in one of the three lower levels of consciousness.

My top ten values

In Figure 1.2, I show how the model can be used by mapping my own top ten values to the Seven Levels of Consciousness. You can do the same at www.valuescentre.com/pva. The box following Figure 1.2 contains the report that was generated by this free assessment.

You can see from this report that my values are distributed across all seven levels of consciousness. My main focus is at the self-actualizing and integrating levels of consciousness.

Figure 1.2: My top ten values.

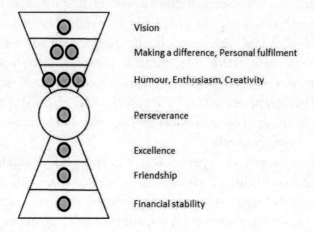

Vision

Making a difference, Personal fulfilment

Humour, Enthusiasm, Creativity

Perseverance

Excellence

Friendship

Financial stability

REPORT R. BARRETT

You have chosen positive values at each level. This indicates that you are able to lead a balanced and fulfilled life. From the values you selected it is clear that you are a person for whom meaning is important. You have a strong set of moral standards that are important in how you treat others and how you wish to be treated.

Your values show:

- A gift for thinking imaginatively and using your skills to produce new ideas to help you make positive change in the lives of others.
- Living with a passionate, upbeat, fun-loving approach is important to you.
- You appreciate high standards of quality and are driven to maintain these in all aspects of your life.
- Remaining in control of your finances and ensuring that you are not over-stretched provide you with comfort.
- Having meaningful close relationships with others is important in your life.

- Demonstrating determination and resolution to follow through ensure that you are able to fulfil your aims.
- It is important for you to have meaning and a sense of contentment in your life.
- You see possibilities where others cannot and you have an understanding of the steps needed to get there.

The type of values you selected indicates that your individual capabilities are most important to you. From your choice of values you also demonstrate care for the greater good.

What does measuring consciousness mean?

Before exploring the Seven Levels Model and its uses, I think it is important to spend some time understanding what it means to "measure consciousness".

Between the moment we are born and the time we reach physical maturity, we all pass through the same three stages of psychological development: surviving, conforming and differentiating. During these stages of development we learn to satisfy what Abraham Maslow referred to as our basic or "deficiency" needs. We get anxious if these needs are not met, but once they are met, we no longer pay much attention to them.

If we progress through these stages of development normally without significant psychological trauma, when we reach our thirties, we begin to feel a pull towards the adult stages of psychological development: individuating, self-actualizing, integrating and serving. During these stages we learn to satisfy what Abraham Maslow referred to as our "growth" needs. Once we experience the sense of meaning and joy our growth needs bring, we want more.

At the same time as we are growing "vertically", becoming more fully who we are by giving expression to the deepest levels of our being, we are also growing "horizontally", acquiring the knowledge, skills and experience we need to live in more complex environments as we move through our infant, childhood, teenage and young adult years. If we fail to

> *The model of psychological development described here differs from most other models in one important way: it looks at development through the lens of the ego-soul evolutionary dynamic.*

grow horizontally—master the skills necessary to live in increasingly complex environments—we will inhibit our ability to grow vertically.

There are many models that focus on adult psychological development, each of them describe evolutionary vertical development in slightly different ways.[2] The model of psychological development described here, the Seven Levels Model, differs from most other (academic) models in one important way: it looks at development through the lens of the *ego-soul evolutionary dynamic*, the growth and development of the motivations of the ego, the progressive but normally subtle influence of the motivations of the soul over the motivations of the ego, and the unfoldment of the motivations of the soul.

The stages of ego development

The stages of psychological development you pass through in your formative years—surviving, conforming and differentiating, are *not* optional: every person experiences these stages of development on their journey to physical and mental maturity. What you are learning during these stages of development is how to become a viable independent adult in your cultural framework of existence. These are the stages of development where we learn to satisfy our "deficiency" needs. The aspect of our personality that grows and develops during these stages of development is the ego. By the time you reach your late twenties, your ego will be fully activated.

How well you mastered your ego development will depend, to a large extent, on the degree and nature (positive and negative) of the parental programming and cultural conditioning you experienced during your infant, childhood and teenage years. If you grew up without too many negative experiences, without forming any significant fear-based subconscious beliefs, you will naturally feel a pull towards the individuation stage of development.

The stages of soul unfoldment

Unlike the first three stages of psychological development, the adult stages of development are in a certain manner of speaking "optional." They are not so much thrust on us by the biological and societal exigencies of becoming an adult, as the first three stages of development are; they appear as subtle inner feelings of wanting more from life and finding answers to questions, such as Who am I? and Why am I here? Aligning your ego motivations with your soul motivations may entail making hard choices and courageous decisions that cause you anxiety, worry or suffering.

The adult stages of psychological development (stages of soul unfoldment) begin at the individuating stage. The individuating stage of development usually occurs in our twenties or thirties.

Individuating requires you to do two things. First, let go of the aspects of your programming and conditioning that do not reflect who you truly are: the values and beliefs you do not resonate with at the level of your soul. Second, learn how to release any conscious or subconscious fears you may have about meeting your deficiency needs. Only when you have accomplished these two tasks, will you be ready to move to the self-actualization stage of your development.

If you are unable to repair the flaws or inadequacies of your ego development—deal with the painful memories of the negative parental programming and cultural conditioning you received in your formative years that keep you anchored in one of the three lower levels of consciousness—you may find it difficult to move through the individuation stage of your development without coaching or therapeutic help.

If, on the other hand, you were fortunate enough to have benefited from a higher education, been brought up by self-actualized parents in a liberal democracy, and had a chance to travel the world, you will probably find your passage through the *individuating* stage of your development to the self-actualizing stage relatively uncomplicated.

Self-actualization involves focusing on and developing your innate gifts and talents—the interests, activities or work you are passionate about. Once you embark on your self-actualization—when you make the commitment to grow—you will find yourself supported in ways you could never have expected. If for any reason you are blocked or prevented from manifesting your gifts and talents, you will be unable to move to the integrating and serving stages of your development.

Obstacles to growth

The biggest obstacles to your growth are your conscious and subconscious fears—the fears you learnt in your formative years that prevent you from meeting your deficiency needs, and the fears you may have about making changes to your life that could disturb the carefully managed dependencies that you rely on to satisfy those needs. You may also find yourself embedded in a culture—family, organizational, community and/or societal—with a world view that actively suppresses or discourages individuation.

The cultural world views we are embedded in are described by the model known as Spiral Dynamics.[3] A discussion of how different world views support or suppress our psychological development can be found in Chapter 6 of my book, *Evolutionary Coaching,* published in 2014.[4] For the sake of convenience, I have included the conclusions of this chapter in Annex 2 of this book.

If you do not live in a liberal democracy, have not benefited from a higher education and have not had the opportunity to travel the world, then the chances are you will not feel the need to individuate and you will ignore any pull you may feel to move in that direction.

You will be relatively content living in the community and social milieu of your childhood and teenage years, never questioning who you are at a deeper level, and never pursuing any promptings to examine your life, your beliefs or your values. Only if you experience a psychological trauma or depression that leads you to question the meaning and purpose of your life will you feel an incitement to ask yourself "Who am I?" and "Why am I here?"

Measuring consciousness

Based on this understanding of the stages of psychological development and levels of consciousness, we can reach some preliminary conclusions about what "measuring consciousness" means: first, measuring consciousness involves determining *what stage of psychological development you have reached*; and second, determining *what stages of psychological development you have passed through where you still have unmet needs.*

The needs you have at the stage of development you are at, and the unmet needs from the stages of development you have passed through, will determine your motivations. These, in turn, will tell you what you value and where your consciousness is focussed. The motivation of the stage of development you have reached will be your primary motivation, and the motivations of the stages you have passed through, that you have not yet mastered, will be your secondary motivations.[5]

If you have any significant secondary motivations, arising from your unmet deficiency needs, they will always take precedence in your mind over your primary motivation. The reason our secondary motivations take precedence is because evolution has taught us to subconsciously examine what is happening in our external environment first through the lens of our fears, and only when our security and safety is assured, do we then explore what is happening in our external environment for opportunities to meet our other needs. For a detailed account of how to identify your primary and secondary motivations please consult my book entitled *Evolutionary Coaching.*

Stages of psychological development

An overview of the seven stages of psychological development is shown in Table 1.1 and a detailed description of each stage can be found in Annex 3.

The first column of Table 1.1 identifies the stages of psychological development. The second column indicates the age range when each stage of psychological development begins to become important. The third column describes the developmental task associated with each stage of psychological development. The fourth column identifies the motivations associated with each stage of psychological development, and the fifth column lists the value priorities at each stage of psychological development.

The age ranges given in the second column are approximate but are generally applicable to people of all races, religions and cultures. It is possible to accelerate your psychological development to a certain degree (by a few years) if you were brought up by self-actualized parents living in a culture with a liberal world view. Although it is relatively rare to find people who have accelerated their psychological development, they could become more prevalent in coming generations as more parents self-actualize and more countries embrace the values found in liberal democracies.

Table 1.1: Motivations and value priorities at each stage of psychological development.

Stages of psychological development	Approximate age range of each stage of development	Overview of developmental task	Motivations (Need requirements)	Value priorities
Serving	60+ years	Fulfilling your destiny by caring for the well-being of humanity and/ or the planet.	Satisfying your need to lead a life of service to others.	Compassion, humility, future generations, ecology, social justice.
Integrating	50-59 years	Aligning with others who share the same values and purpose to create a better world.	Satisfying your need to make a difference in the world.	Collaboration, empathy, mentoring, coaching.

Self-actualizing	40-49 years	Becoming more fully who you really are by leading a values- and purpose-driven life.	Satisfying your need to find meaning and purpose in life.	Authenticity, integrity, fairness, trust, transparency.
Individuating	20 to 39 years	Letting go of the aspects of your conditioning that no longer serve you.	Satisfying your need for freedom and autonomy.	Independence, continuous learning, adaptability.
Differentiating	8 to 19 years	Distinguishing yourself by honing your natural skills and talents.	Satisfying your need for respect and recognition.	Achievement, status, continuous improvement.
Conforming	2 to 8 years	Keeping safe and secure by staying loyal to your kin and community.	Satisfying your need for love, and belonging.	Belonging, friendship, harmony, loyalty, rituals.
Surviving	Birth to 2 years	Staying alive and physically healthy in the best possible conditions.	Satisfying your physiological needs.	Survival, security.

The lower three stages of development represent the evolution of our ego's motivations and the upper three stages represent the unfolding of our soul's motivations. The individuating stage of development is where we begin to align the beliefs of the ego with the values of the soul, and the self-actualizing stage of development is where the ego learns to embrace the interests and passions of the soul.

At any moment in time, no matter what age you are at, your value priorities are a reflection of your needs and your needs are a reflection of your motivations. Consequently, as you grow and develop, your values priorities will change in accordance with your changing needs.

Figure 1.3 shows how the proportion of people choosing the value of friendship as one of their top ten values varies by age in the UK. What is apparent, as you might expect, is that younger people place a higher priority on friendship than older people who are more likely to be married and have children.

Figure 1.3: Proportion of people choosing the value of friendship at different age ranges.

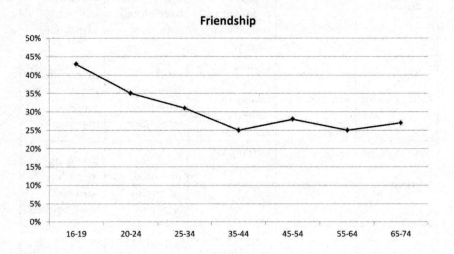

Ego motivations and soul motivations

In order to understand how we grow and develop vertically through the different stages of psychological development, we have to understand the mechanisms at play in the ego-soul evolutionary dynamic. To do this we must establish a clear understanding of what the ego is and what its motivations are, and what the soul is and what its motivations are.

Your ego is a field of conscious awareness that identifies with your body; it believes it lives in a three-dimensional physical reality. It has two primary objectives and three overriding needs. The ego's objectives are to survive and protect itself. To achieve these objectives it needs to keep the body—the vehicle it identifies with—and the bodies of those it cares about, secure and safe (surviving); it needs to love and be loved so that it can feel a sense of belonging (conforming); it needs to be recognized by others for its gifts and talents so it can feel a sense of self-worth (differentiation). These needs are described in the lower part of the fourth column in Table 1.1.

When your ego is able to satisfy these needs you feel at ease; energetically, you feel a sense of internal stability. When the ego is unable to satisfy these needs you feel anxious; energetically, you experience a sense of internal instability.

Your soul is a field of conscious awareness that identifies with your energy field; it lives in a four-dimensional energetic reality, in the space-time continuum of the quantum level of existence. Einstein was familiar with this concept. He once said:

> *The non-mathematician is seized by a mysterious shuddering when he hears of four-dimensional things, by a feeling that is not unlike the occult. But there is no more commonplace statement than the world in which we live is a four-dimensional continuum.*[6]

Your soul—who you really are—is an individuated aspect of the universal energy field. Because it knows it cannot die, the soul has no fears. The soul never loses consciousness. When we die, the soul simply withdraws its attention from the three-dimensional physical world to the four-dimensional energetic world. It inhabits this world even while it is projecting itself into our three-dimensional physical reality.

> *Your soul is a field of conscious awareness that identifies with your energy field; it lives in a four-dimensional energetic reality, in the space-time continuum of the quantum level of existence.*

The soul has two primary objectives and three overriding needs. Its objectives are to lead a values- and purpose-driven life. To achieve these objectives the soul needs the ego to align with its values (individuating) and purpose (self-actualizing), live out its purpose by collaborating with others to make a difference in the world (integrating), and lead a life of selfless service for the good of humanity and the planet (serving). These needs are described in the upper part of the fourth column in Table 1.1.

Two worlds

The reality of the ego-mind is based in what Ervin Laszlo, the Hungarian-born philosopher of science, refers to as the M-dimension (the observable, manifest, three-dimensional world), and the reality of the soul-mind is based in what he refers to as the A-dimension (the unobservable, potential, four-dimensional world), what Einstein refers to as the four-dimensional continuum. The A-dimension (Akashic dimension) is a universal field of information and potentiality which is in constant interaction with the M-dimension.

> *The M-dimension and the A-dimension are related diachronically (over time) as well as synchronically (at a given point in time). Diachronically, the A-dimension is prior: it is the generative ground of the particles and systems of particles that emerge in the M-dimension. Synchronically, the generated particles and systems of particles (in the M-dimension) are linked with the A-dimension through bidirectional interactions.*[7]

Even though the ego-mind derives its sense of reality from focussing its attention on the M-dimension (physical reality), it exists in the same energy field as the soul-mind in the A-dimension (energetic reality).

Another way of looking at this is to say your energy field (your personality) contains three minds: the body-mind that regulates the internal systems of the body so we can maintain internal stability, the ego-mind and the soul-mind. Whatever is going on in your ego-mind significantly impacts your energy field and thereby affects your body-mind and soul-mind. When your ego generates fear-based thoughts, you will feel a sense of heaviness, separation and instability. This is because fear has a low frequency of vibration, whereas love, the energy that emanates through the soul, has a high frequency vibration; it feels light and stable. It feels connecting rather than separating. When you are constantly operating with fear-based thoughts you will tend to suffer from neuroses and your body may become sick.

When the fear-based energies of the ego-mind are closely juxtaposed with the love-based energies of the soul-mind, your energy field will experience internal instability. This shows up in our lives as emotional pain: anxiety, stress, anger, frustration, impatience, and in some situations, where you have bottled up your emotions over long periods of time, rage.

> *As you shift the locus of your identity from your ego to your soul, you will experience less fear in your life and your energy field will shift to a higher frequency of vibration.*

As you shift the locus of your identity from your ego to your soul—as you pass through the individuation and self-actualization stages of development—you will experience less fear in your life and your energy field will gradually shift to a higher frequency of vibration. You will feel happier, more joyful and more content. You may even experience moments of bliss.

What all this means is that your experience of the M-dimension is conditioned by the degree of alignment of your ego-mind with your soul-mind in the A-dimension; most importantly, by the level of fear that exists in the ego-mind and the level of alignment of the ego's motivations with the soul's motivations. As the conscious and subconscious fear-based beliefs of your ego-mind decrease, the opportunity for your soul-mind to influence your decision-making increases.

This leads us to the conclusion that the "optional" part of the journey of the evolution of consciousness, which corresponds to the adult stages of psychological development (from the individuating to serving stages), depends on three conditions:

- The degree to which you are able to separate yourself from the beliefs of your parental programming and cultural conditioning that do not align with the values of your soul.
- The degree to which you are able to master your ego's conscious and subconscious fear-based beliefs.
- The degree to which your soul-mind is able to live a values- and purpose-driven life in the three-dimensional physical reality of the M-dimension; the degree to which you are able to embrace your true self and your unique self.[8]

The body-mind

As already mentioned, in addition to the ego-mind and the soul-mind, we also have a body-mind. The body-mind represents the conscious awareness of the atoms, molecules, cells and organs of the body. The purpose of the body-mind is to keep the body in a state of internal stability by responding to changes in its external physical environment. For example, when the temperature rises, we sweat: the evaporation of the water molecules on our skin cools us down. This ability of the body to self-regulate is known as "homeostasis". The body-mind, like the ego-mind and soul-mind, is contained within the human energy field.

The energy field

The part of your energy field related to the body-mind is known as the etheric field; the part of the energy field related to the ego-mind is known as the emotional field; the part of the energy field related to the soul-mind is known as the spiritual field. The etheric field that surrounds and penetrates the physical body is surrounded by the emotional field, which in turn is surrounded by the spiritual field. The energy field of the ego-mind is separated from the energy field of the soul-mind by the ego's mental field, a dispassionate logical information processing facility.[9]

Each layer of the energy field has a different frequency of vibration. The lowest frequencies occur in the etheric field, and the highest frequencies occur in the spiritual field. Whenever our energy fields are out of alignment—electromagnetic imbalance—we feel discomfort or unease in our bodies.

The mental field—let us call it the rational mind—is available to the ego-mind and the soul-mind, however, the ego-mind can only access the mental field when it is calm and relaxed. When it is in a state of agitation or excitement (emotion) it is unable to make use of the mental field. Rationality flies out of the window when the energy associated with emotionality takes over our mind space.

Because of its close proximity to the body-mind (etheric field), the vibrational frequencies of the ego-mind (emotional field) have a direct influence on how the body-mind operates: whatever is happening in the ego-mind is immediately felt in the energy field of the body-mind. When the ego-mind is operating from fear, the body-mind reacts by releasing chemicals that prepare the body for fight or flight. When fear reaches a semi-permanent state, because of anxiety or stress, the continuing production of these chemicals becomes harmful to the body's health, eventually resulting in physical dis-ease and sickness.

Getting back into alignment, means bringing your electromagnetic energy field into a state of internal stability. We do this by finding ways to realign the vibrational frequency of the ego-mind with the vibrational frequency of the soul-mind. This is called personal mastery or leading self. The key elements of leading self and personal mastery programmes are learning how to manage your emotions, and learning how to practice mindfulness and meditation.

When the ego-mind is in alignment with the soul-mind—when the ego shares the same values and motivations as the soul, and operates with minimal levels of fear—the body experiences a state of internal stability; you feel fit and healthy, and experience a sense of inner well-being.

Notes

1. For more information go to www.valuescentre.com.
2. For a list of development models, see Ken Wilber, *Integral Psychology: Consciousness, Spirit, Psychology, Therapy* (Boston: Shambhala Publications), 2000, and Dr. Alan Watkins, *Coherence: The Secret Science of Brilliant Leadership* (London: Kogan Page), 2014.
3. Don Beck and Christopher Cowan, *Spiral Dynamics: Mastering Values, Leadership and Change* (Malden: Blackwell Publishing), 1996.
4. Richard Barrett, *Evolutionary Coaching: A Values-Based Approach to Unleashing Human Potential* (London: Fulfilling Books), 2014, pp. 76–88.
5. For a full discourse on primary and secondary motivations and how to identify them, see *Evolutionary Coaching: A Values-based Approach to Unleashing Human Potential* by Richard Barrett.
6. R. W. Clarke, *Einstein: the Life and Times* (New York: World Publishing), 1971, p. 159.

7. Ervin Laszlo, *The Self-actualizing Cosmos: The Akasha Revolution in Science and Human Consciousness* (Rochester: Inner Traditions), 2014.

8. Marc Gafni, *Your Unique Self: The Radical Path to Personal Enlightenment* (Tucson: Integral Publishers), 2012.

9. This is a simplified explanation of the human energy field. For a more detailed description see: Barbara Brennan, *Hands of Light: A Guide to Healing Through the Human Energy Field* (New York: Bantam Books), 1987.

2

Understanding Consciousness

With this brief overview of the Seven Levels Model and the ego-soul evolutionary dynamic, we are now ready to explore my two objectives for writing this book:

1. To explain the theory behind the Seven Levels Model.
2. To show how the Seven Levels Model can be used to measure the consciousness of individuals and groups.

I would like to focus on four questions:

1. Why is it important to measure consciousness?
2. What are the attributes of consciousness that allow it to be measured?
3. What is consciousness and how does it evolve?
4. How could a metric of consciousness be deployed?

I will tackle the first two questions in this chapter, the third question in Chapter 3, and the last question in Chapters 4, 5, and 6.

Why is it important to measure consciousness?

The benefit of being able to measure something is that you can manage it. Measuring enables you to learn what you need to do, and what you need to avoid or stop doing, to get more of what you want. Measuring gives you the ability to locate yourself on a scale. We are all familiar with scales. We use them to help us monitor our weight, test our IQ and manage our vital indicators such as blood pressure and heart rate.

I believe the consciousness scale I am proposing in this book enables you to find out:

1. What stage of psychological development you have reached in your life.
2. What stages of psychological development you have passed through that you have not fully mastered.
3. As a consequence of these, what primary and secondary levels of consciousness you are operating from.

In addition, the consciousness scale can be used to measure the levels of consciousness the cultures you are embedded in are operating from and to what extent you are aligned with these cultures.

The hope

The great hope that developing a metric for human consciousness brings is that we can make the evolution of consciousness conscious, not just at the individual level, but also at the organizational, community and societal levels too. The ability to measure consciousness gives you the opportunity, if you so wish, to manage your own evolution and the evolution of the human group structures in which you are embedded.

> *The great hope that developing a metric for consciousness brings is that we can make the evolution of consciousness conscious.*

This is exactly what the leaders and organizations who work with the Cultural Transformation Tools do. Each year they measure the culture (consciousness) of their organizations by carrying out a Cultural Values Assessment, track their own personal evolution, by carrying out a Leadership Values Assessment, and based on the feedback they receive, make personal and cultural changes that result in an overall improvement in their own performance and the performance of their organizations.

This shows up in the following year's assessments as either a greater concentration of positive values at a particular level of consciousness (horizontal growth) or as a shift of values to higher levels of consciousness (vertical growth).

The basics of measurement

In order to measure consciousness, we must do two things. First, we must develop a scale that we can measure against: a model of consciousness. Second, we must identify the attributes of consciousness that enable us to determine where we are on that scale. Only when we have defined these two—a scale and the attributes—do we have a measuring system. This means we must arrive at a clear understanding of what consciousness is, and what attributes or qualities are associated with growth and regression in consciousness. In other words, what are the factors that cause us to move up or down the consciousness scale?

What are the measurable attributes of consciousness?

Let's start our inquiry into what the measurable attributes of consciousness are by looking at some popular conceptions of consciousness.

First, it is generally agreed that consciousness evolves in stages, and that developing your consciousness means two things: *mastery*, learning how to operate successfully at a particular stage of psychological development, and *growth*, shifting from one stage of psychological development to a "higher" stage. There is an underlying assumption that if you are unable to master the requirements for operating at one stage, you will find it difficult to successfully shift to the next higher stage.

Stages and levels

Before looking at what "higher" means in terms of consciousness, let us first explore in a little more detail the difference between stages and levels of consciousness.

The simplest way I can explain this is to say that we grow in stages (of psychological development), and we operate at levels (of consciousness). All things being normal, the level of consciousness we operate from corresponds to the stage of psychological development we have reached.

I think it is useful here to repeat what I said earlier about threats and "peak" experiences. When we are faced with what we consider to be a negative change in our circumstances or a situation that threatens our internal stability or external equilibrium in some way—anything that brings up fear—we may temporarily shift to operating from one of the three lower level of consciousness. Alternatively, when we have a "peak" experience—an experience of euphoria, harmony or connectedness of a mystical or spiritual nature—we may temporarily shift to a higher level of consciousness.

When the threat or peak experience has passed, we usually return to the level of consciousness that corresponds to the stage of psychological development we were at before the experience occurred. In rare situations, a peak experience may have a lasting impact, causing us to shift to a higher stage of psychological development and operate from a higher level of consciousness.

Similarly a "negative" experience, if it is traumatic enough, and particularly if it occurs in your childhood and teenage years, can impede your future psychological development by causing you to be anchored, through frequent subconscious triggering of the traumatic memory, into in one of the three lower levels of consciousness.

What does "higher" mean

Now let's get back to the determining what "higher" means in the context of consciousness.

The first attribute of higher consciousness that most students of consciousness agree on is an expanded sense of identity: more inclusivity, less separation, more connectedness. Whenever you assume a larger more inclusive identity, your sense of self expands to include others who share the same identity. We always operate from self-interest, but the self that has the interest now has an expanded identity.

Identity

When you shift from being single to having a family, you expand your sense of identity to include your spouse and children. When you find a job that you like, in an organization where you feel comfortable, you expand your sense of identity to include the colleagues you work with (your team). As you move into the realms of management or leadership, you may start to identify with the organization itself. Those of you with a religious persuasion may identify with your religious group. When you are part of a minority race in a community, you may identify with those people who share your heritage.

One of the changes that occurs when we shift to a new level of identity is we start caring for the well-being of the members of the group we identify with. When you identify with your family, you care about the well-being of the members of your family. When you identify with a work team, you care about the well-being of the members of your team. When you identify with your organization, you care about the well-being of the members of your organization. When you identify with your religion, you care about the well-being of the people who share your faith. When you identify with your race, you care about the well-being of the people who look like you, dress like you and speak your language. When you identify with everyone on the planet, you care about the well-being of humanity. When you identify with the planet, you care about the well-being of all living species and their natural environments. Each time you expand your sense of identity, you don't just feel an increase in your sense of connection you expand your sense of self.

If you fail to care for the members of the groups you identify with (belong to or are embedded in), and focus on your personal self-interest rather than the group interest, you may find yourself ignored, marginalized or excluded from the activities of the group: You will become increasingly isolated and feel a sense of separation from those around you.

Complexity

Another meaning we often give to "higher" in the context of consciousness is the ability to operate in increasingly complex frameworks of existence. As we progress from being infants, to children, to teenagers, young adults, and adults, the physical and social frameworks of our existence become increasingly larger and more complex. In order to successfully survive and thrive in these larger, more complex environments, we must develop more complex minds; we must increase our breadth perception (knowledge) and depth perception (understanding), not just about our surroundings and how things work, but also about the people who are members of the groups we identify with in these expanded frameworks of existence.

Some of the natural outcomes of expanding our sense of identity— being more inclusive and developing more a complex mind—are that we increase our level of maturity, we learn to handle ambiguity, we learn to think in longer-term time horizons, we become less fearful, more trusting, more at ease with uncertainty, and more confident in our abilities to cope with whatever life throws at us. The progressive development of these attributes naturally leads us to higher stages of psychological development and levels of consciousness. The most important of these attributes are increasing our feelings of connectedness and decreasing our feelings of separation. To pursue these objectives, you must regard everyone you meet as an equal and learn to overcome your fear of conflict.

For me, these popular conceptions of the evolution of human consciousness provide a good starting point for understanding how consciousness evolves, but they do not get to the heart of the matter. I believe if we really want to understand what consciousness is and how it grows, then we have to take a deep dive into understanding how consciousness evolved in our three-dimensional physical framework of existence.

How did consciousness evolve?

According to scientists, everything that exists in our universe originated from a "big bang" that occurred around fourteen billion years ago.[1] After that, it was all about evolution: the evolution of energy into matter, matter into living organisms, and living organisms into creatures. One of those creatures—Homo sapiens—is now attempting to carry the baton of evolution to the next level, to make the concept of humanity palpable.

When I say everything in the universe had its origins fourteen billion years ago, I literally mean everything, including not only the physical world of atoms, cells, and Homo sapiens, but also the energetic world of instincts, thoughts, feelings, beliefs and values. Indeed, evolution would not have happened if the faculties we attribute to the physical brain (data gathering and information processing) had not evolved in parallel with the faculties we attribute to the mind (meaning-making and decision-making).

Consequently, we find ourselves living in two worlds: Laszlo's M-dimension—the three-dimensional physical world of the body, the tangible part of our existence, and Laszlo's A-dimension—the multi-dimensional energetic world of the mind, the intangible part of our existence.

If the big bang theory is correct, then it follows that the physical world emerged from the energetic world. Not only did energy precede matter, we know, thanks to Einstein, that energy and matter are related ($E=mc^2$). Energy is equivalent to matter, times the speed of light, squared. In other words, energy is the fundamental backdrop to our physical universe.

A world where space and time become interwoven in a single energetic continuum, not only challenges our physical senses, it also challenges our beliefs. We are so conditioned to our physical reality that any other form of reality seems ludicrous. However, when you understand the implications of particle physics and quantum theory, the idea that we live in a strictly physical world starts to get a bit wobbly.

Modern science tells us that at the quantum level of existence, energy can exist either as electrically charged particles or as waves of information. The reality of the particle is three-dimensional: it has specific physical properties. The reality of the wave of information is four-dimensional: it is an energy field unbounded by space and time. Only when an observing consciousness is present does the wave of information (or potentiality) collapse into a specific form.

When the observing consciousness is the ego, the reality we experience will align with the beliefs of the ego. When the observing consciousness is the soul, the reality we experience will align with the values of the soul. In other words, the three-dimensional world of physical form is dependent on the four-dimensional world of the mind and which pole of consciousness (ego or soul) we identify with and operate from.

To appreciate the differences between these two worlds—our three-dimensional reality and our four-dimensional reality—I am going to suggest we do a mind experiment. Let us explore the differences that exist between two-dimensional reality and three-dimensional reality, and then based on the results, try to draw some conclusions about the possible relationship between our three-dimensional physical reality and our four-dimensional energetic reality.

Five finger exercise

Take a sheet of paper and lay it down on a flat surface. Imagine that there is a very small person living on the surface of this paper in what is known as "Flatland". For this person, the world has length and breadth, but no height. In other words, this person operates in a world of two-dimensional awareness (she cannot perceive height). Along comes a human being with three-dimensional awareness (this person can perceive height) and places the fingers of one hand on the paper, on the surface of Flatland.

Imagine now, that the person living in Flatland is out for a morning stroll. When passing this place yesterday, she noticed nothing unusual. Suddenly, overnight, five separate circles have appeared (the projection into two-dimensional consciousness of the five fingers). The two-dimensional being is mystified by the appearance of the five circles. She calls her friend, a two-dimensional scientist, and asks him to explain the nature of the five circles. The scientist explores the five circles using his two-dimensional logic.

His experiments show that if he puts a force on one circle, it will move and eventually appear to drag the other circles with it (although the fingers of the hand are separate they are connected, but in a dimension of awareness [height] that the two-dimensional scientist cannot perceive). The two-dimensional scientist repeats his experiments. He builds equations to verify the relationship of the circles to each other and before too long he believes that he knows everything there is to know about the five separate circles. He publishes a paper about the five separate circles and calls a meeting of the academy of two-dimensional scientists to show them his discovery. The two-dimensional scientists repeat the experiments and get very similar results. Everyone in the two-dimensional world believes they know all there is to know about the five separate circles.

Viewed from the perspective of three-dimensional awareness, we know that these are not five separate circles. They are five connected fingers forming part of a living organism. The two-dimensional beings are completely unaware of this larger picture. They believe the five circles to be physically separate, but somehow linked, probably through some type of energetic force field. They have no sense of the connection that exists at a higher dimension of awareness.

This is exactly the situation we find ourselves in with regard to the fourth dimension of consciousness. We have countless experiences that appear unconnected, but in reality are linked, and have their cause in the fourth or higher dimensions of consciousness. Some we try to explain with our three-dimensional logic, this is the domain of science, and some are simply inexplicable, these we classify as paranormal, synchronistic, magical, religious or miraculous experiences. We use these classifications to cover up our ignorance because we do not have a full understanding of the linkages that exist at the higher dimensions of consciousness where these experiences originated.

When we focus our awareness exclusively on the third dimension we are focussing on a world of symbols and effects, the origins of which lie elsewhere. The average person relying on his three-dimensional senses is unaware of the greater connectivity or unity that exists in the higher dimensions of consciousness.

Let us use another analogy. Take a comb and cover up the top half. What you see are the unconnected teeth of the comb. You see separation. When you uncover the top half of the comb you can see that the teeth are joined together at a higher level. You see connectedness; you see the unity of the comb. Indeed, the teeth of the comb without the higher-level connection would fall apart and could not fulfil a useful purpose.

As human beings, this is how we are. What we perceive in our three-dimensional awareness are separate human beings (teeth of the comb). When we raise our awareness to a higher plane of consciousness, we can see the connection at the energetic level; we are all individuated aspects of the same unifying energy field. Just as it is difficult to understand the meaning and purpose of the separate teeth, until we are aware that they belong to a comb, so, too, it is difficult for us to understand who we are until we become aware that we are all individuated aspects of a universal energy field; souls connected through our energy fields in the fourth and higher dimensions of consciousness.

This field of connectedness is referred to by the renowned psychiatrist and psychotherapist, Carl Jung, as the collective unconscious: collective, because it belongs to all of us, and unconscious, because it is not directly accessible through conscious thought.

There is one more point we should consider about the five finger exercise. Just as the two-dimensional beings experiencing the phenomena of "the five circles" did not suspect that the circles were controlled by the mind of a three-dimensional being, so, we, in our three-dimensional world, are unaware of the control that our souls exercise in our lives from the fourth dimension of consciousness.

What appear to be random events or chance encounters may be due to purposeful connections occurring between souls at a higher dimension of consciousness, which we are simply unaware of. These are usually described as synchronistic events. I prefer to call them soul prompts.

Carl Jung described synchronicity as "unconnected events with a common meaning". In my experience, if you dig deep enough, you will almost always find that chance events and encounters have a meaning that in some way furthers the soul's purposes. It is as if the synchronistic experiences are communications from our souls at the fourth dimension of consciousness that are designed, not only get our attention, but to convey important messages to us about taking some form of action in our three-dimensional plane of existence.

The limitations of our senses

Why are we not more aware of our four-dimensional energetic realty? The answer is simple. We are not aware of it because of the limitations of our physical senses. Just as the being living in two-dimensional awareness could not sense height, we as three-dimensional beings only have a vague awareness of the four-dimensional energetic world of our souls.

We have five physical senses that we use to inform us of what is happening in the physical world around us. Everything we can personally know about our external physical world is experienced through these senses. However, the physical senses that the human species (and all other creatures) have developed are extremely limited in terms of the frequencies of vibration that we can sense, and consequently, are at odds with much of what science tells us. There are vast ranges of sound that we cannot hear and there are vast ranges of radiation we cannot see or feel. It is as if we are trapped within a body that only allows us to experience a very small part of reality, the three-dimensional world of physical forms.

The truth is we live in a multi-dimensional energetic world, but because of the limitations of our senses, we only perceive three of these dimensions. We can state that *three-dimensionality and physical form are not properties of the world, but are properties of our senses.* Everything in our physical universe is composed of matter, and at the same time is contained within an energy field that is "invisible" to our physical senses.[2]

The universal stages of evolution

Evolution began by energy coalescing into particles that became viable and independent in the physical framework of existence. These particles then bonded together to form protons, neutrons and electrons that "cooperated" with each other to form atoms. From this stable platform, life on Earth began: atoms learned how to become viable and independent in the framework of their existence then bonded together to form molecules, which cooperated with each other to form complex molecules and cells.

Once cells had learned how to become viable and independent in their framework of existence—manage their internal stability and external equilibrium—they bonded with each other to form organisms, and organisms cooperated with each other to form complex organisms and creatures (See Table 2.1).

Table 2.1: Three universal stages of evolution.

Planes of being	Sub planes
Creatures (Homo sapiens)	Regional groups and global groupings.
	Bands, tribes, city-states, nations.
	Humans.
Cellular plane (Eukaryotic cell)	Complex organisms.
	Organisms.
	Cells.
Atomic plane (Carbon atom)	Complex molecules.
	Molecules.
	Atoms.
Energetic plane	Quantum reality

One of those creatures—Homo sapiens—is now learning how to become viable and independent (manage its internal stability and external equilibrium) in its framework of existence, and how to bond with other members of the species to form bands, tribes, city-states and nations; nations are learning how to cooperate with each other to create higher-order regional entities such as the European Union and global entities such as the United Nations.

From Table 2.1 we can see that each plane of being can be divided into three sub-planes differentiated by scale and complexity: the plane of being of an individual entity; the plane of being of the group structures that are formed by that entity; the plane of being of groups of group structures of that entity, some of which evolve to become a larger entity and the starting point for the next plane of being. I call this evolutionary progression "the three universal stages of evolution".

We see displayed in this evolutionary progression, in the overall schema and at each plane of being, the characteristics of increasingly higher levels of consciousness: an increase or expansion in the sense of identity (inclusivity) of the entity, and an increase in size and complexity of the entity's framework of existence requiring a commensurate increase in the complexity of the entity's mind. For evolution to have progressed, the entities and group structures at one plane of being had to provide a stable platform for the entities and group structures at the next plane of being.

In order to understand how and why these different entities and their group structures at each plane of being decided to share a common identity, we have to take a close look at the causation that leads to the three universal stages of evolution.

Stage 1: Becoming viable and independent

In order to survive, the fundamental entities at each plane of being (particles, atoms, cells and creatures) have to learn how to become viable and independent (be able to maintain internal stability and external equilibrium) in their frameworks of existence. If an entity cannot learn how to do this it will quickly perish (cease to exist in the physical world and disintegrate into its component parts at a lower plane of being). Ultimately, through this process, everything returns back to energy.

Stage 2: Bonding to form a group structure

When the framework conditions of entities become more complex and life threatening[3] they respond by bonding with other viable independent entities to share resources and form a more resilient group structure with a shared sense of identity.

In order for this to happen, the entities that form part of a group structure have to learn how to bond with each other so they can work together for the good of the whole. In other words, individual entities have to expand their sense of identity to include the other entities in the group structure.

Once entities have bonded—developed a high level of internal cohesion by increasing their capacity for unified decision-making— and a group structure has been formed with its own sense of identity, the ability of the group structure to survive and prosper depends on the ability of the entities forming the group structure to share resources and work together for the common good.

Entities that fail to put the needs of the group structure ahead of their own needs (such as cancer cells) not only threaten the survival of the group, they also threaten their own survival and the potential survival of every entity that is part of the group. In other words, when individual entities in a group structure focus too much on their own "self-interest" rather than the good of the whole—when they feel a sense of separation—the viability of the group structure is compromised.

This is why we have rules and laws in our human social world. The rules and laws provide a framework of acceptable behaviours that allow human group structures to create internal stability. Without the general acceptance of these rules and laws and an expanded sense of identity, our families, organizations, communities and nations would descend into a state of chaos.

Whenever individual entities focus on their own self-interest rather than the interest of the group structure, internal tensions are created that lead to cultural entropy. Cultural entropy is the level of disorder or dysfunction that occurs within a human group structure due to a lack of internal cohesion. When cultural entropy (the self-interest of the entities that make up the group structure) reaches a high level, the group structure will break down into its component parts and will cease to exist.

Stage 3: Cooperating to form a higher order entity

When the framework conditions of a group structure become more complex and "life threatening", group structures respond by cooperating with other group structures to share resources and create a higher order entity (an enlarged group structure), which is more resilient than any of the group structures could be on their own.

In order for this to happen every entity and every group in the larger group structure has to share resources and work together for the good of the whole; they have to shift to a higher level of identity. When the group structures that form a higher order entity focus too much on their own "self-interest" rather than the good of the whole—when they fail to shift to a higher level of identity—the viability of the higher order entity is compromised.

Once a higher order entity is formed and has developed a strong level of internal cohesion—capacity for unified decision-making—the ability of the group structures to survive and prosper now depends on the ability of the higher order entity to survive and prosper. This is true at every plane of being.

The ability of a cell which is part of an organ to thrive and prosper depends on the ability of the organ of which it is a part to survive and prosper. Similarly, the ability of a human being to survive and prosper depends on the ability of the group structures it is part of (clan, tribe, organization, community or nation) to survive and prosper. This is why identity is so important to survival. If you identify with your clan, tribe, organization, community or nation, the members of these groups will not only care about you, they will also share recourses.

Individuals and group structures that fail to put the needs of the higher order entity ahead of their own needs—fail to adopt an expanded identity—not only threaten the survival of the higher order entity, they also threaten the survival of the group structures to which they belong. In other words, when individual group structures in a higher order entity focus too much on their own "self-interest" rather than the good of the higher order entity, the viability of the higher order entity will be compromised.

Based on the universal stages of evolution, we can clearly see that *bonding and cooperating are evolutionary imperatives.* Without them, evolution could not have happened and higher forms of consciousness (identity) would not have been possible.

In other words, evolution progresses not by entities becoming the fittest, but by becoming the most inclusive and stable. There is a definite evolutionary advantage in being able to expand your consciousness (your sense of self or self-identity) to include others; in other words, there is an evolutionary advantage in advancing your psychological development.

This idea is backed up by the latest scientific research. Using game theory, two evolutionary biology researchers found that: "evolution will punish you if you're selfish and mean. For a short time and against a specific set of opponents, some selfish organisms may come out ahead. But selfishness isn't evolutionary sustainable."[4]

This finding has significant implications for our personal psychological evolution and the cultural evolution of the species. If we want to evolve it is vitally important that we learn how to bond and cooperate with others, not just in difficult times but also in good times. To survive and prosper, we need to focus on the interest of the group structures in which we are embedded rather than our own self-interest.

Based on the theory of the universal stages of evolution we can conclude that evolution will only continue to progress if we, the members of the species known as Homo sapiens, can learn how to bond with each other to create human group structures that cooperate with each other to solve the problems of humanity.

This leads us to the fundamental question: "Why are some entities able to bond and cooperate more easily than others?" If we can find the answer to this question, we will not only be able to identify the attributes that make evolution possible, but the attributes that allow consciousness to expand.

> *Evolution will only continue to progress if we can learn how to bond with each other to create human group structures that cooperate with each other to solve the problems of humanity.*

The attributes of consciousness that make evolution possible

Among all the different entities that existed at each plane of being, there was only one entity that was able to form a stable physical and energetic platform (starting point) for the next stage of evolution. At the atomic plane, it was the *carbon atom*. At the cellular plane, it was the *eukaryotic cell*. Now in the plane of being of creatures, it is *Homo sapiens*.

If you ask the question "What attributes do these specific entities (the carbon atom, eukaryotic cell and Homo sapiens) possess that enabled them to become the platform for the next stage of evolution?", you will begin to see a pattern emerging. The answer to the question is quite simply, *the ability to bond and cooperate.*

The carbon atom

The *carbon atom* is one of the most stable elements because it has four electrons available for covalent bonding. Covalent bonding is the strongest form of chemical bonding. It involves the *sharing* of electrons (resources) between pairs of atoms.

Because of the stability afforded by this type of structural bonding, carbon was able to form durable complex molecules with many different elements. Consequently, carbon is the second most abundant element in the human body after oxygen and the fourth most abundant element in the universe after hydrogen, helium and oxygen. There are more compounds of carbon than all the other elements put together. Carbon atoms form the chemical basis of almost all forms of life known to man.

The eukaryotic cell

The *eukaryotic cell* differs from its evolutionary predecessor, the prokaryotic cell, not just because it is larger, but because of its internal structure and its ability to form communities of shared awareness. Unlike the prokaryotic cell, which has its "organelles" located in the cell membrane, the eukaryotic cell has its "organelles" (each organelle being a specialized prokaryotic cell) in the interior of the cell. This enables the cell membrane of the eukaryotic cell to grow in size and develop more sophisticated communication systems than the prokaryotic cell. Consequently, the eukaryotic cell can bond and cooperate with other eukaryotic cells to build organisms and specialized physiological structures such as muscles, bones, and organs. Eukaryotic cells are the cellular basis of all life because they are able to communicate with each other.

Homo sapiens

Homo sapiens is potentially the third link in the chain of evolution because it has a greater propensity for bonding and cooperation than any other creature. Not only do we have the most sophisticated communication system (language), we are also able to organize ourselves into communities of shared identity and shared interest.

In order to survive and prosper in our globally interconnected world, we must shift from focussing on our own self-interest, to focussing on the interest of the group structures we belong to, and our group structures must shift from focussing on their self-interest, to focussing on the interests of the higher order group structures that represent our common humanity.

This message is vitally important for all of us at this point in history, particularly for our leaders, because the problems of existence we are facing are global but the structures of governance we have for dealing with them are primarily national. We will only be able to evolve if we put aside our self-interest and pay more attention to our collective interest. In other words, focus on the values that promote bonding and cooperation.

Notes

1. There are other theories about how the world we live in originated. Like Laszlo's theory mentioned earlier, many of them are built on two worlds: a manifest physical world and an energetic world of emergent potentialities.

2. Article by Richard Conn Henry, *The Mental Universe*, Nature (Vol. 436) 7 July 2005.
3. Life threatening means challenging the ability of the entity or group structure to maintain its internal stability and external equilibrium.
4. Article, Nature Communications, *Evolutionary instability in zero-determinant strategies demonstrates that winning is not everything,* by Christophe Adami and Arend Hintze, published 1 August 2013.

3

Defining Consciousness

Now we have a clearer idea of the mechanisms that drive the evolution of consciousness—becoming viable and independent, bonding to form a group structure, cooperating to form a higher order entity—and their relationship to identity, cohesion and inclusion, let us get to grips with the problem of defining consciousness.

For evolution to have progressed from the energetic plane all the way through to the plane of creatures and the emergence of Homo sapiens, every entity and every group structure in the chain of evolution had to develop a way of maintaining its internal stability and external equilibrium in its framework of existence. In other words, they had to find ways of becoming viable and independent under their normal operating conditions (managing their internal stability and external equilibrium). Without this ability, entities and group structures would not have survived, and would not have become stable platforms for subsequent planes of being to build on.

What this means is that every entity and group structure at every plane of being had to be able to sense changes in its environment, determine whether the changes were threatening to its survival, and if they were, take some form of action to adapt to these changes, or if the changes were too threatening, take evasive action.

If an entity or group structure could not adapt or take evasive action, then the only option left for survival—remaining present in our three-dimensional physical world—was for the entity or group structure to bond or cooperate with other entities or group structures to share resources in temporary or permanent alliances and thereby increase their collective resilience. In other words, evolution favours those entities that are:

1. Adaptable in terms of identity.
2. Able to bond and/or cooperate with other entities for the purpose of sharing resources.

Without some form of awareness (consciousness) and an ability to decide how to respond to changes in their environment (mind), entities at every plane of being could not have taken actions to preserve their internal stability when changes occurred in their external environments.

Antonio Damasio, author, and internationally known Professor of Neurology, puts it this way: *Homeostasis is the key to the biology of consciousness.*[1] In other words, consciousness is the mechanism that enables living entities to maintain their internal stability.

What I am saying goes further than Damasio's statement: the concept of homeostasis does not stop at the biological level; it goes all the way down to the atomic level and beyond to the energy field. *Ergo,* "homeostasis" and consciousness are intimately linked. Without some form of conscious awareness, "homeostasis"—the ability to maintain internal stability in a changing external environment—would be impossible not just at the cellular plane of being but also at the atomic plane of being. In other words, below self-reflective human consciousness (what Damasio calls extended consciousness) there are other forms of consciousness (what Damasio calls core conscious), the consciousness of cells and their group structures as well as the consciousness of atoms and their group structures.

Based on this we can define core consciousness as *awareness with a purpose* and the primary purpose of core consciousness is *to support an entity or group structure in maintaining or enhancing its internal stability and external equilibrium so it can stay present in our three-dimension physical reality.* This applies to all entities and all group structures on all planes of being.

It follows, therefore, that the primary purpose of *extended* consciousness *is to support human individuals or group structures in maintaining their internal stability and external equilibrium at the stage of psychological development they have reached and at the stages of development they have passed through where they still have unmet needs.*

Ultimately, however, when one realises that everything in our three-dimensional physical world depends for its existence on our four-dimensional energetic world, we can say the purpose of consciousness (core and extended) is *to support an entity or group structure in maintaining or enhancing the internal stability and external equilibrium of its energy field by satisfying the needs of the entity at the stage of psychological development it has reached, and the needs of the entity at the stages of psychological development it has passed through that it has not yet mastered.*

Each time we shift to a new stage of psychological development, we have to begin again to learn how to manage our internal stability and external equilibrium in the new more complex framework of existence. Only when you have successfully learned how to manage your internal stability and external equilibrium at every stage of psychological development can you be considered to be a full spectrum individual.

Mind and consciousness

There are two major implications that can be drawn from the earlier statements: first, wherever you have an entity or group structure that is attempting to maintain its internal stability and external equilibrium, you have consciousness; second, wherever you have consciousness you have a mind. Mind and consciousness are synonymous because consciousness is a property of mind. There can be no conscious without a mind.

Consciousness needs a mind to make decisions that lead to behaviours that enable an entity to maintain its internal stability and external equilibrium in the face of threats, and mind needs consciousness to identify threats to its existence as well as opportunities for thriving, increasing its internal stability and external equilibrium so that an entity can become more resilient (more skilled at coping with threats and satisfying its needs).

How mind decides what actions to take to stay present (alive) in our three-dimensional physical world depends on the plane of being the mind exists at and its ability to store "memories" about how to react or respond to changes in its environment that have been successful in the past.

At the physical or body level, we use memories stored in the energy field of our DNA molecules to help us stay alive. DNA-encoded reactions (instincts) operate like beliefs. For example, if the body-mind/brain complex notices in its awareness an information pattern (energetic signature) of an event or situation labelled "a", it will respond by doing "x"; if it notices in its awareness an event with an energetic signature labelled "b", then it will respond by doing "y"; where "x" and "y" are species memories that generate emotions and actions that the entity "believes" will give it the best chance possible to maintain or enhance its internal stability and external equilibrium when encountering events "a" or "b" based on past species experiences.

At the individual human level, in addition to our species memories, we also have autobiographical memories to help us survive. These memories operate in exactly the same way as our species memories. If we notice an incoming information pattern that reminds us of threat to our internal stability or external equilibrium we have previously experienced, we will react in the manner that gave us the best chance possible of maintaining or enhancing our internal stability and external equilibrium in the past.

The purpose of consciousness

Based on this we can draw the following conclusions:

1. The primary purpose of consciousness is survival; staying present in the three-dimensional physical world of matter.
2. In order for consciousness to fulfil this purpose it must be associated with a mind that is (a) conscious and (b) has a sense of its own identity.

The energy field of the mind must be able to distinguish what is "me" and "not me", what is internal and external, if it is to bond to form a group structure, then it must be able to adapt its sense of "me" and "not me"—its identity—to include other entities with which it wants to bond.

What we learn by studying the different planes of being that comprise the human body is that the concept of identity is expandable. Even though atoms, molecules, cells and organs have a sense of what is internal and external, and know how to keep themselves in internal stability and external equilibrium, they are able, at the same time, to assume a higher level of identity—the identity of the body—for the purpose of staying alive. In other words, like human beings, they have multiple identities. They maintain internal stability by identifying with themselves, and they maintain external equilibrium by identifying with other similar and larger entities. To do this, all the entities involved must share a common purpose.

> *If the energy fields (minds) of the atoms, molecules, cells and organs of our bodies did not share a common purpose (staying alive) and identity (the body), they would not be able to work together for the common good in the same energy field.*

If the energy fields (minds) of the atoms, molecules, cells and organs of our bodies did not share a common purpose (staying alive) and identity (the body), they would not be able to work together for the common good in the same energy field. Cells that feel a sense of separation—stop working for the common good, focus on their self-interest and compete for resources, are called cancer cells.

Studies have revealed that a significant number of cancer patients suffer from unresolved anger towards other people; a condition of the mind that creates a sense of separation. This suggests that most cancer begins in the mind before it manifests in the body. Separation is the antithesis of bonding and cooperation, and therefore creates a way of being that is not evolutionary sustainable.

Based on the foregoing, we can state that every building block of the human body is conscious, all the way down from the organs to the cells, to the molecules, to the atoms and their particles. Even when we are unconscious or asleep, the body is conscious: it is constantly self-regulating based on the feedback it is receiving from its external environment.

If the body-mind is unable to self-regulate for any reason, let's say because the conditions in its physical environment go beyond the limits of what it can manage, then it signals its distress to us—the higher order entity that it is serving and identifies with—through pain or discomfort. The pain or discomfort we feel originates in the energy field of the body-mind and is felt in the energy field of the personality mind. When we get such a signal, we attempt to alleviate the pain or distress in the body-mind by taking actions which the body-mind is unable to do without our cooperation. For example, if the body gets too hot, the body-mind causes us to sweat and the discomfort we feel signals to us that we should find ways to cool off and increase our intake of fluids.

The ego-mind

If we assume for a moment that our full potentialities are contained within the quantum energetic field of the soul—our true identity and the aspect of our being that remains forever conscious and transcends the death of the body—then we can ask the question, what is it that blocks us from expressing these potentialities? The answer is quite simple: the beliefs of the ego-mind, particularly its fear-based beliefs. When we allow these beliefs to rule our decision-making, we choose safety over growth and we limit the potential of the soul.

Abraham Maslow puts it this way:

> *We can consider the process of healthy growth to be a never ending series of free choice situations, confronting each individual at every point throughout his (or her) life, in which he (or she) must choose between safety and growth, dependence and independence, regression or progression, and immaturity and maturity.*[2]

The ego-mind is the aspect of your personality that has been conditioned, through the experience of identifying with a human body and its three-dimensional perception to living in a physical world. The ego will do everything in its power to protect the body's physical integrity. It believes in scarcity, and considers life to be a zero-sum game: I win and you lose; you win and I lose. Consequently, the ego readily embraces the concept of self-interest and the need to compete for resources.

Because the ego identifies with the body, it believes in death. The ego believes when the body dies it will no longer exist. Consequently, the consciousness of the ego-mind, like the consciousness of the body-mind, is constantly focussed on survival, safety and protection; finding ways to maintain its internal stability and external equilibrium.

The ego is totally absorbed in making the best of its three-dimensional existence: it not only wants to survive, it also wants to thrive. Thriving for the ego-mind means finding ways to accumulate more material resources, get more love, and gain more recognition. When it is able to satisfy these needs it feels happy. The ego is unaware of its quantum energetic reality, and the world of the soul.

Those who have been pronounced clinically dead and have come back to life (three-dimensional physical awareness) can attest to this fact. During their "death" experience they did not experience a loss of consciousness. They simply experienced a different reality. Many people recount experiences where they left their body and were no longer reliant on their normal three-dimensional physical perception (senses).

What I believe they experienced was the energy field of the soul, because they let go of the energy field of the ego-mind and the body-mind. Such experiences not only convince people that they cannot die, they take away their ego's fears about surviving. This can result in a permanent shift to a higher stage of psychological development and a higher level of consciousness.

The soul-mind

Your soul is the reason you exist in this three-dimensional physical reality. Your soul-mind is a field of conscious awareness that exists in the energetic realm of the fourth dimension of reality, beyond space and time, in the quantum electromagnetic energy field. Your soul is an individuated aspect of the universal energy field from which everything that exists in our physical world derives its existence. In other words, the soul-mind is the aspect of your personality that identifies with the human energy field, whereas the ego-mind is the aspect of your personality that identifies with the human body.

The soul lives in abundance and sufficiency. It is at ease with uncertainty and thrives on change. Because it is comprised of the fundamental energy of existence (spirit), it cannot be created or destroyed and it cannot lose consciousness. At death, your soul's consciousness continues. The energy field of your soul-mind lets go of the body-mind and ego-mind so that it can be fully present in a higher dimension of reality.

Your soul projected itself into your physical body shortly after your conception and imbued every atom and cell in your body with

> *The will to survive is the soul's will to be present in physical form in our three-dimensional reality.*

the will to survive. We can state that *the will to survive*, which is found in the body-mind of every living creature, and the ego-mind of every human being *is the soul's will to be present in physical form in our three-dimensional reality.*

The reason your soul incarnated into your body is to bring the soul experience of being into three-dimensional physical reality. In pursuit of this objective, your soul has two strategic objectives that your ego can choose to align with or not: first, to lead a values-driven life, and second, to lead a purpose-driven life.

Your soul cannot fulfil these objectives unless your ego is able to shift into energetic alignment with your soul; shift its sense of identity from the physical body to the energy field of the soul. Your ego must follow the path of the universal stages of evolution: Become viable and independent (individuate); bond with the soul (self-actualize); and cooperate with other souls (integrate).

Understanding internal stability

In order to understand how the ego-mind aligns itself with the soul-mind, we must explore further the topic of internal stability. The idea I want to explore is this: what we refer to as internal stability at one plane of being is external equilibrium at the previous or lower plane of being.

This means that every mind at every plane of being relies on the minds of entities at lower planes of being to achieve internal stability (cohesion). This is what creates a stable platform for evolution. In the meantime, while this is happening, the mind at the higher plane of being is focussing on its external equilibrium.

The mind of the atom relies on the minds of its particles to support its internal cohesion while it focusses on its external equilibrium in the world of atoms; the molecule relies on the minds of its atoms to support its internal cohesion while it focusses on its external equilibrium in the world of molecules; and so on all the way up the chain of being. Human group structures rely on individual human beings to support their internal stability (through bonding), while they focus on their external equilibrium (through cooperating) in the world of human group structures.

The ego-soul evolutionary dynamic

Similarly, the soul-mind relies on the ego-mind and its sub-personalities to support its internal cohesion while it focusses on its external equilibrium in the world of souls.[3] Any form of upset—disturbance in the ego-mind (the emotional field)—causes the energy field of the soul-mind (the spiritual field) to become internally unstable.

At any moment in time, the feelings we are experiencing are a reflection of the status of the ego-soul evolutionary dynamics in our energy field; more particularly, the degree to which the fear-based beliefs of the ego-mind are affecting the vibrational frequency of the soul's love-based energy field.

To understand the principle factors that affect the ego-soul evolutionary dynamic—the energetic relationship between the ego-mind and the soul-mind—we need to dig deep into the fundamental principles of evolution. We need to understand how an entity achieves internal stability. Based on the preceding discussion we can identify three conditions that must be met for an entity to experience internal stability:

1. The lower order entities must identify with the higher order entity.
2. The lower order entities must have unanimity of purpose, which is the same purpose as the higher order entity.
3. The lower order entities must be energetically compatible with each other and the higher order entity.

If we take the human soul as an example, internal stability occurs when the ego identifies with the soul, the ego shares the same purpose as the soul, and the ego embraces values that enable the soul to bond and cooperate with other souls to further the process of evolution.

If your ego does not shift it sense of identity to align with the soul, does not align with the soul's purpose and does not embrace values that promote bonding and cooperation with other souls, then your energy field will never achieve internal stability and you will never be able to evolve to the higher stages of psychological development.

If we take a human organization as an example, internal stability occurs when employees share the same sense of identity, work towards a common purpose and are energetically aligned. Let us say for the moment the shared sense of identity is the organization, the unanimity of purpose is the organization's mission, and the energetic alignment is an agreement among all members of the organization to operate from a common set of values.

We can see that values are significantly important to the evolution of consciousness. Without shared values we cannot achieve internal stability, and without internal stability we cannot evolve in consciousness because achieving internal stability is a prerequisite for evolving to the next stage of psychological development.

What are values?

According to sociologists, "values" are *the ideals and customs of a society towards which the people have an effective regard*. I prefer to define values in a more pragmatic way: *Values are a shorthand method of describing what is important to us individually or collectively (as an organization, community or nation) at any given moment in time*.

From a fourth-dimensional perspective, we can define values as *the energetic drivers of our aspirations and intentions*. Values are "energetic" because they belong to the intangible world of the mind and our energy field.

From the soul's perspective, we can say values are *the principles we need to live by to support bonding and cooperation; the values that promote evolution*.

Values are different from beliefs. The values that promote bonding and cooperation are universal; they transcend contexts. Beliefs, on the other hand, are context-dependent. They depend on the world views of the culture you are brought up in and the parental programming you received in your formative years. Consequently, values unite people and beliefs tend to separate people. This is particularly true of religious and ideological beliefs.

Positive values are the universal guidance system shared by all souls, whereas beliefs are the context-related guidance system of the ego. When you shift from the control of your personality from your ego to your soul, you automatically move from belief-based decision-making to values-based decision-making. This shift means that you can effectively throw away the rulebooks you learned when you were young. Every decision you now make will be sourced from what you consider to be "right action"—actions that are fully aligned with who you really are—your soul self, and values that promote bonding and cooperation (evolution). Values-based decision-making allows you to create a future that resonates deeply with who you really are. It creates the conditions that allow your authenticity and integrity to flourish.

If you want to live in soul consciousness, every critical decision you make in life should pass the values test. If a decision you want to make seems logical but goes against your soul-based values—does not promote or prevents bonding and cooperation—you should not proceed.

The way you know a decision is not aligned with your soul's values is because of how it makes you feel; the impact it has on your energy field. When you make decisions that are sourced from fear, you promote separation and your energy field takes on an increased negative charge: You feel a sense of heaviness. When you make decisions that are sourced from love, you promote cohesion and your energy field takes on an increased positive charge; you feel a sense of lightness.

I am not saying there is no place in our lives for conscious belief-based decision-making based on logic or rational thinking. There is. What I am saying is that before arriving at a final decision about how to deal with a situation, you should always explore how your decision makes you feel. If it does not feel right—does not promote bonding or cooperation—then you should think again. As previously stated, decisions based on self-interest, in the long run, do not promote evolutionary sustainability.

Notes

1. Antonio Damasio, *The Feeling of What Happens* (New York: Vintage Books), 1999, p. 40.
2. Ibid., p. 48.
3. Why do I say "world of souls"? Because that is who we are! We do not have souls, we are souls! We live in a world of souls attempting to bring soul consciousness into our three-dimensional physical reality.

4

Measuring Personal Consciousness

Having defined a framework for measuring human consciousness and identified how your sense of identity (inclusivity) expands through various stages, from your ego identity to your soul identity, let us now explore the mechanics of measuring consciousness. To this end we will need to define two new concepts: personal entropy and cultural entropy.

Personal entropy is the amount of fear-driven energy that a person expresses in their day-to-day life as measured through their interactions with, or behaviours towards other people. Personal entropy arises from the subconscious fear-based beliefs that we learn during the surviving, conforming and differentiating stages of our psychological development. These represent our ego's unmet needs—not having enough, not being loved enough, and not being enough—also known as secondary motivations. When we are making decisions based on fear-based beliefs, we are focussed on our own self-interest. As a result, we promote separation.

Cultural entropy is the amount of conflict, friction and frustration that people encounter in their day-to-day activities that prevent a human group structure (team, organization, community or nation)

> *Personal entropy is the amount of fear-driven energy that a person expresses in their day-to-day life as measured through their interactions with other people.*

from achieving its peak performance. The main source of cultural entropy is the fear-based actions and behaviours of the current leader(s) and the institutional legacy of past leaders; the fear-based beliefs embedded in the structures, policies, systems and procedures of the organization.

At the individual level, personal entropy creates disturbances in your personal energy field, which prevents your ego from bonding and cooperating with your soul. At the group level, cultural entropy creates disturbances in the group's energy field, which prevent members of the group from bonding and cooperating with each other.

Cultural Transformation Tools

The measuring instruments I am going to present are described in several of my previous books. Collectively, these measuring instruments are known as the Cultural Transformation Tools (CTT). A description of the latest version of these measuring instruments can be found in *The Values-Driven Organization: Unleashing human potential for performance and profit*[1] or by going to www.valuescentre.com.

Since their inception, the CTT have been used to measure the consciousness of more than five thousand organizations, four thousand leaders, and twenty-four nations. More than five thousand people in sixty countries have been accredited in the use of these tools.

You can measure your own consciousness by doing a free self-assessment at www.valuescentre.com/pva. This assessment gives you your perspective on your values. These are the values you believe you operate with or the values you aspire to.

In order to find out where you *actually* are on the spectrum of consciousness, rather than your potentially biased perception of yourself, you must do a feedback assessment; find out how others see you. In a feedback assessment 15–20 people are asked to pick ten values/behaviours that reflect how you operate. They choose from a list (template) of 80–90 words or phrases. The values/behaviours included in the template represent all levels of consciousness and contain positive as well as potentially limiting (negative) values.

Positive values include words such as friendship, family, accountability, trust and making a difference. These are values that promote connection, bonding and cooperation. Potentially limiting values include words such as control, blame, manipulation, status-seeking and arrogance. These are values that promote separation and conflict and create personal entropy.

The top ten highest scoring values and the distribution of all the values chosen by the assessors are plotted against the Seven Levels of Consciousness model. The level of personal entropy is arrived at by calculating the proportion of votes for potentially limiting values chosen by all the assessors.

Measuring the consciousness of a high entropy individual

Figure 4.1 shows the results of a feedback assessment obtained for an individual operating with high personal entropy. The number alongside each value represents the number of votes for this value by the assessors. The total number of assessors in this case was fifteen. An (L) next to a value indicates a potentially limiting value. The white dots indicate the placement of potentially limiting values and the grey dots represent the placement of positive values.

Figure 4.1: Levels of consciousness of an individual with high personal entropy.

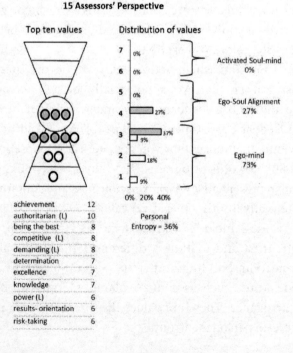

15 Assessors' Perspective

Top ten values

achievement	12
authoritarian (L)	10
being the best	8
competitive (L)	8
demanding (L)	8
determination	7
excellence	7
knowledge	7
power (L)	6
results- orientation	6
risk-taking	6

Distribution of values

Personal
Entropy = 36%

In the opinion of his assessors this individual is focussed in his ego-mind, 73% of his values are located in the first three levels of consciousness (ego-mind); 27% of his values are at the ego-soul alignment levels. There are no values at the activated soul-mind levels. The level of personal entropy (36%) is arrived at by adding up the proportion of votes for potentially limiting values at the first three (ego) levels of consciousness (9%+18%+9%).

This person has started the process of individuation (primary motivation) but has not yet reached the level of self-actualization. What is blocking the evolutionary progress of this person is his high level of personal entropy related to his secondary motivations. The potentially limiting values in the top ten values chosen by the assessors suggest this person is achievement-focussed: he is an authoritarian, highly competitive, demanding and power seeking. All of these values promote separation rather than inclusion.

The degree to which a person is fully aware of who they are and how they are perceived by others can be gauged by asking the person whose consciousness is being assessed to also pick ten values about how they see themselves operating. Their view of their own values is then compared to their assessors' view of them.

Figure 4.2 shows how the person assessed in Figure 4.1 views himself, alongside the assessor's perspective (shown in Figure 4.1). The percentages in parenthesis on the extreme right-hand side of the figure are the individual's own assessment of their distribution of values compared to the assessors.

Figure 4.2: Comparison of how a high-entropy individual sees himself and how he is seen by his assessors.

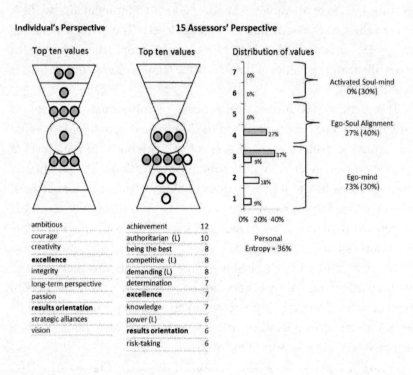

Individual's Perspective	15 Assessors' Perspective	
Top ten values	Top ten values	Distribution of values

ambitious	achievement	12
courage	authoritarian (L)	10
creativity	being the best	8
excellence	competitive (L)	8
integrity	demanding (L)	8
long-term perspective	determination	7
passion	**excellence**	7
results orientation	knowledge	7
strategic alliances	power (L)	6
vision	**results orientation**	6
	risk-taking	6

Activated Soul-mind 0% (30%)
Ego-Soul Alignment 27% (40%)
Ego-mind 73% (30%)

Personal Entropy = 36%

What is immediately obvious from this example is the mismatch between how the person sees himself and how others see him; this person does not have a realistic view of himself. His ego projects a false persona. He is living behind his ego mask. He views himself as operating at higher levels of consciousness than his behaviours would suggest to his assessors.

He has two matching values between how he sees himself and how others see him: *excellence* and *results orientation*. He does not attribute any personal entropy to himself (no potentially limiting values in his top ten) but his assessors' indicate he is operating with a very high level of personal entropy (36%).

Measuring the consciousness of a low entropy individual

Figure 4.3 shows the results obtained for an individual with low personal entropy.

Figure 4.3: Levels of consciousness of an individual with low personal entropy.

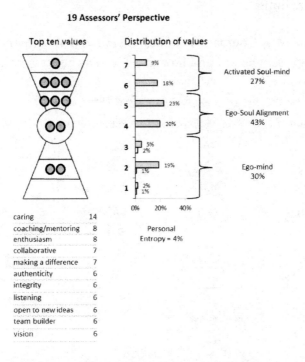

In the opinion of the nineteen assessors, this individual is focussed in the higher levels of consciousness: 43% of the assessor's votes are at the transformation and internal cohesion levels of consciousness (ego-soul alignment) and 27% are at the making a difference and service levels of consciousness (activated soul-mind). This person is well advanced in their self-actualization and has a low level of personal entropy (4%).

Figure 4.4 compares how this person sees herself compared to the feedback from 19 assessors. The percentages in parenthesis on the extreme right-hand side of the figure are the individual's own assessment of their distribution of values. In this case, compared to the previous one, there is a much stronger correlation between how people see this person and how she sees herself: there are four matching values in the top ten: *listening, open to new ideas, team builder* and *vision*.

What is striking about this person compared to the previous example is that she has a slightly more modest perception of who she is compared to her assessors. Interestingly, neither of the two people is aware of how they are coming across to others: she underestimates herself, while he overestimates himself.

Figure 4.4: Comparison of how an individual with low entropy sees herself and how she is seen by her assessors.

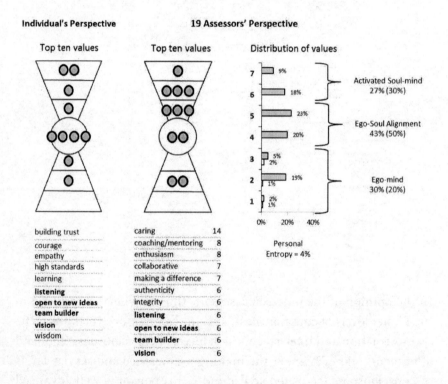

The main difference between these two examples—the high entropy and low entropy individuals—is that the first individual is primarily operating from the ego levels of consciousness and the second individual is primarily operating from the ego-soul alignment levels of consciousness and above.

Let us now take a look at how we can measure the consciousness and cultural entropy of an organization.

Note

1. Richard Barrett, *The Values-Driven Organization: Unleashing Human Potential for Performance and Profit* (London: Routledge), 2013, pp. 119-144.

5

Measuring Organizational Consciousness

The technique involved in measuring the consciousness of a human group structure such as an organization, a community or a nation is slightly different from the way we measure individual consciousness. We ask people who are part of the group structure to pick ten values/behaviours from a template of 80–90 words or phrases that best describe who they are, how their group operates (current culture) and how they would like their group to operate (desired culture). For the moment, let us focus on the results of the question about how the group operates (current culture).

The values included in the template that people pick from represent all levels of consciousness and contain positive as well as potentially limiting (negative) values.

Positive values might include words such as financial stability, accountability, openness, trust and making a difference. Potentially limiting values might include words such as control, blame, hierarchy, fire-fighting and bureaucracy. The top ten highest scoring values and the distribution of all the values chosen by the people in the group are then plotted against the Seven Levels of Consciousness Model and the level of cultural entropy is calculated. This is the proportion of all the votes for potentially limiting values chosen by the individuals in the group.

The template can be customized for a particular group: this involves putting words in the template that represent values/behaviours that are specific to the context of that group.

A high cultural entropy, low alignment organization

Figure 5.1 shows a typical result for high cultural entropy (fear-driven), low alignment organizations. Eighty managers in this organization were asked to assess the current culture of their organization. The number alongside each value represents the number of votes for it. An (L) next to a value indicates it is a potentially limiting value. The white dots represent the placement of potentially limiting values and the grey dots represent the placement of positive values.

What is immediately obvious from this example is the low level of consciousness and high level of cultural entropy in the current culture of this organization: 73% of the values in are located at the level of the ego-mind; 22% at the level of ego-soul alignment; 5% at the level of the activated soul. Seven of the top ten values in the current culture are potentially limiting values.

Figure 5.1: Levels of consciousness of an organization with high cultural entropy.

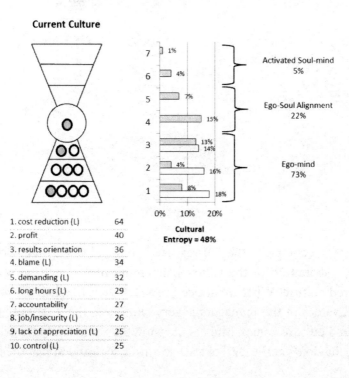

1. cost reduction (L)	64
2. profit	40
3. results orientation	36
4. blame (L)	34
5. demanding (L)	32
6. long hours (L)	29
7. accountability	27
8. job/insecurity (L)	26
9. lack of appreciation (L)	25
10. control (L)	25

Let us now compare the current culture with the managers' desired culture. This comparison is shown in Figure 5.2.

The managers are asking for a significant shift in consciousness. Although none of the top ten values are located at the fifth level of consciousness, 20% of the votes were for values/behaviours at this level, making the total proportion of votes for ego-soul alignment 51%, and for an activated soul-mind 16%.

The top ten values/behaviours requested in the desired culture are all different from the top ten values reported in the current culture. This organization is stuck in a culture of blame. The leaders are demanding and controlling and because of the poor performance there is strong focus on cost reduction. Despite working long hours, people are not appreciated and are feeling insecure about their jobs.

Figure 5.2: Comparison of current culture and desired culture.

Current Culture				Desired Culture	
1. cost reduction (L)	64			1. continuous improvement	40
2. profit	40		Cultural Entropy = 48%	2. customer satisfaction	36
3. results orientation	36			3. accountability	29
4. blame (L)	34			4. coaching/mentoring	28
5. demanding (L)	32			5. leadership development	26
6. long hours (L)	29			6. teamwork	23
7. accountability	27			7. open communication	22
8. job/insecurity (L)	26			8. adaptability	21
9. lack of appreciation (L)	25			9. employee recognition	21
10. control (L)	25			10. information sharing	21

Figure 5.3 compares the self-reported personal values/behaviours[1] and the distribution of the values/behaviours of the managers with the desired culture. What we notice immediately is the distribution of personal values of the managers is very similar to the distribution of the desired culture values. The results show 34% and 33% of votes for values/behaviours at the level of the ego-mind, 53% and 51% at the level

of ego-soul alignment, and 13% and 16% at the level of the activated soul-mind. People want to work in a culture that reflects their personal consciousness.

The most significant difference is at levels 4 (transformation) and 5 (internal cohesion). Whereas their personal values are primarily located at level 5, the level of internal cohesion, the desired culture values are located at level 4. This shows the managers recognize that in order to reduce the level of cultural entropy and the number of potentially limiting values in the current culture, they must first work at the level of transformation (level 4) before working at the level of internal cohesion (level 5). It is from the transformation level that these managers can resolve the issues that are causing the cultural entropy in the organization. This will involve working with the senior leaders to reduce their levels of personal entropy.

Figure 5.3: Comparison of personal consciousness
with desired consciousness.

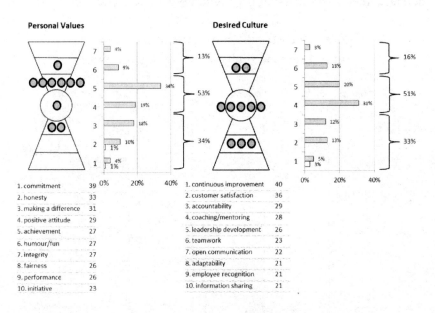

In this example I have mainly focussed on the distribution of values rather than on the actual values themselves. In a normal cultural values assessment we would pay a lot of attention to the actual values in order to determine what needs to be done to transform and improve the performance of the organization (see *The Values-Driven Organization: Unleashing human potential for performance and profit* (July 2013)).[2]

A low cultural entropy, high alignment organization

In my second organizational example, I show the results from typical low cultural entropy, high alignment organizations. This is a small organization of 18 people with 2% cultural entropy, four matching personal and current culture values, and seven matching current and desired culture values. All of these indicate a high level of cultural alignment.

Figure 5.4 shows the distribution of the personal, current culture and desired culture values. What we immediately notice is the high degree of alignment between the levels of consciousness. The strong alignment along with the low level of cultural entropy creates a high level of engagement. This is a highly productive, very successful company.

Figure 5.4: Distribution of consciousness in a low cultural entropy, high alignment organization.

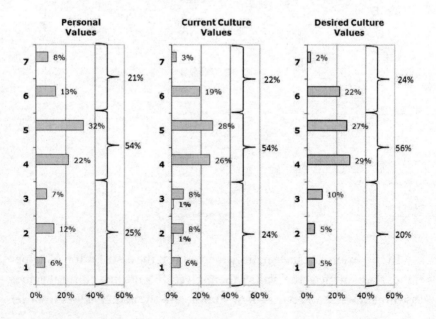

Employee engagement and cultural entropy

In Figure 5.5 I present the results of the research we carried out with Hewitt Associates into the correlation between employee engagement and cultural entropy. Not surprisingly, high cultural entropy leads to low engagement, and low cultural entropy leads to high engagement. Highly engaged employees are not only more productive, they are also more committed to the success of the organization; they are willing to go the extra mile to make sure the organization is successful. For more information, see Chapter 2 of *The Values-Driven Organisation (The impact of values on performance)*.

Figure 5.5: Correlation between employee engagement and cultural entropy.

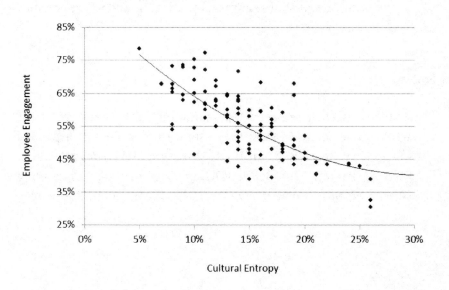

As cultural entropy is a measure of the fear-based attitudes and behaviours that are found in a group culture, we arrive at the conclusion that people work best in a caring, love-based environment rather than a fear-based environment.

Conclusions

Based on the results of thousands of measurements of individuals and organizations we have reached two conclusions:

1. Higher states of consciousness are inversely correlated to personal and cultural entropy (fear-based energy). As the amount of fear-driven energy reduces, the level of ego-soul alignment and soul activation increases.
2. Soul activation on its own does not lead to higher levels of human or organizational performance; the most successful individuals and human group structures are those where attention to the ego's needs is balanced with attention to the soul's needs, and a significant amount of attention is continuously given to working on ego-soul alignment by reducing, and where possible, eliminating fears.

Notes

[1.] As these are their self-reported values, they either represent their actual values or the values they aspire to. The shadow aspect of someone's personality tends not to show up in self-reported values.

[2.] Richard Barrett, *The Values-Driven Organization: Unleashing Human Potential for Performance and Profit* (London: Routledge), 2013.

6

Measuring National Consciousness

A high cultural entropy, low alignment nation

The following data is taken from the UK national values assessment undertaken in 2012. Figure 6.1 shows the distribution of all the votes for personal, current culture and desired culture values. There is very little alignment between who the people are and the values they see in the nation. The level of entropy in the current culture is 59%. There is 6% entropy in the personal values and 4% entropy in the desired culture values. The high level of entropy in the current culture reflects the citizen's perspective on how the country is run.

Figure 6.1: Distribution of consciousness in the UK.

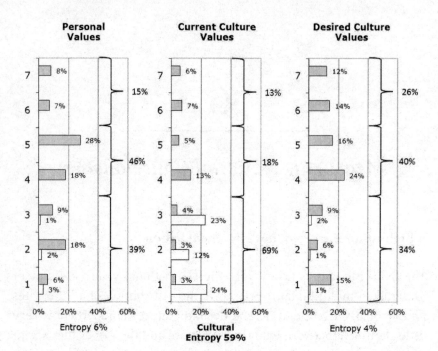

A low cultural entropy, high alignment nation

The following data is taken from the Bhutan national values assessment undertaken in 2008. Figure 6.2 shows the distribution of all the votes for personal, current culture and desired culture values. There is an extremely strong alignment between participant's personal values, the values they see in the nation and the values they would like to see in the nation. The level of entropy in the current culture is 4%. There is 6% entropy in the personal values and 4% entropy in the desired culture values.

Figure 6.2: Distribution of consciousness in Bhutan.

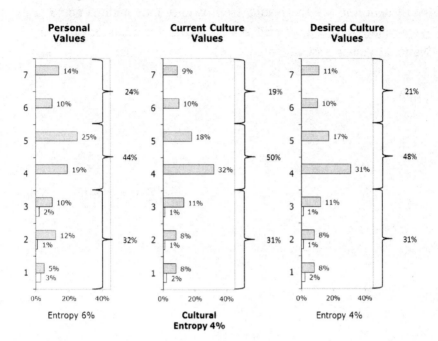

Compared to the UK, the distribution of citizen's consciousness in Bhutan is significantly higher. Of the Bhutanese citizen's personal values, 24% are at the level of soul activation compared to 15% for the UK (personal values). I believe this is due to the strong Buddhist influence found in Bhutan. People from both nations have roughly the same proportion of values at the ego-soul alignment level (46% and 44%).

Even though Bhutan is a developing country without many of the modern conveniences of the UK, the level of ego-driven energy (focus on deficiency needs) among the citizens of Bhutan is smaller than the UK (32% compared to 39%). Compared to the UK, with 5% of values at the level of self-actualization in the current culture, Bhutan has 18%. In some ways this is a surprising result, because Bhutan, at the time the survey undertaken was a kingdom, whereas the UK was a democracy.

These results—the high level of alignment, and the low level of cultural entropy—suggest the people of Bhutan have a strong level of trust in their leaders.

For more information on how to carry out a national values assessment and see the results from twenty-four nations go to http:// www.valuescentre.com/ and search under Products & Services for National Values Assessments (NVA).

ANNEX 1

Overview of the Origins of the Seven Levels Model

The idea for the Seven Levels Model began when I came across Abraham Maslow's hierarchy of needs. It was clear to me when I read Maslow's books that his thinking was ahead of his time: Maslow died in 1970 at age sixty-two, well before the consciousness movement had taken root. As I studied his model, I noticed that with some minor changes, his hierarchy of needs could be transposed into a model of consciousness. I set about making these changes around 1995 and completed them the following year. The correlation between Maslow's model and the Seven Levels Model (Barrett Model) is shown in Table A1.1

Table A1.1: From Maslow to Barrett.

Maslow's Hierarchy of Needs	Barrett's Levels of Consciousness
	7 Service
Self-actualization	6 Making a difference
	5 Internal cohesion
Know and understand	4 Transformation
Self-esteem	3 Self-esteem
Belonging	2 Relationship
Physiological needs	1 Survival

Expanding the concept of self-actualization

The first change I made was to expand Maslow's concept of self-actualization. I wanted to give more definition to our soul's needs (sometimes referred to as our spiritual needs). I achieved this goal by integrating the concepts associated with the states of consciousness described in Vedic philosophy—soul consciousness, cosmic consciousness, God consciousness and unity consciousness—into the seven levels of consciousness model.

According to Vedic philosophy our multi-dimensional minds have the ability to experience seven states of consciousness. The first three—waking, dreaming and deep sleep—are part of everyone's daily experience.

In the fourth state of consciousness (soul consciousness) you begin to recognize that you are more than your ego and your physical body. You begin to identify with the values and purpose of your soul and its energetic reality. You can experience this state of consciousness through meditation. During meditation the body and its neurological systems become fully relaxed. At the same time your mind basks in the peace that lies beyond space and time.

Beyond soul consciousness is a fifth state consciousness, known as cosmic consciousness. In this state of consciousness you remain totally identified with your soul at all times, not just when you meditate. You live in a fear-free state of mental and physiological functioning. In this state, you effortlessly fulfil your desires while simultaneously supporting the interests of others. You operate on the principle of self-referral. That is to say, you are able to live your life to its fullest without ever feeling dependent on the approval of others. You are the master of your destiny because you have become the servant of your soul.

At the sixth state of consciousness, known as God consciousness, you become aware of the deep level of connection between your soul and all other souls—there remains only the finest sense of separation between you and others. You begin to realize that beyond the soul level of consciousness there are no "others"—we are all individuated aspects of the same universal energy field. When I give to you, I am giving to another aspect of myself. When I criticize you, I am criticizing another aspect of myself.

At the seventh state of consciousness, known as unity consciousness, you become one with all there is. The self fuses with the self aspect of every other form of creation in total oneness. There is no separation between the knower and the object of knowing. As far as I am aware, this represents the highest state of consciousness that humans can attain.

As you progress through these different stages of consciousness, you experience an increasingly higher and more inclusive sense of identity.

Whereas, we all experience the first three states of consciousness— waking, dreaming and sleeping—almost every day of our lives, the frequency of our experiences of the higher states of consciousness depends on the stage of psychological development we have reached— the degree to which we have learned how to release our conscious and subconscious fears and live a values-driven and purpose-driven life.

As we make progress on mastering our basic physical and emotional needs, letting go of our subconscious fear-based beliefs, and thereby liberating our souls, we gain more frequent access to the higher states of consciousness. You will recognize these moments quite easily because you will be overcome by feelings of love, joy or bliss. You may feel energy surging or tingling through your body in moments of resonance, or you may feel a profound sense of connection to another person or to the world in general. Sometimes these experiences will last for a short moment, sometimes for several seconds, and if you are lucky, for several days.

I will always remember the profound sense of joy that descended on me two hours after my mother died. I had been with her every day during the last year of her life. She was bedridden and unable to take care of herself. It felt like the joy I was experiencing was her joy at being released from her physical body. She had wanted to leave her body for several months. She kept on saying to me, "Why can't I die like my sisters?"—they all died suddenly. The joy of my mother's release from her physical body stayed with me for almost two weeks, only diminishing gradually after her burial.

You may have had a similar experience in your life, or you may have had several such experiences. Seeking these experiences has never been

71

my goal. I prefer to see them as gifts of grace from my soul. They give me a sense of connection to the fourth dimension of consciousness (and beyond), and make me feel that my life is real, valuable, and therefore has meaning.

Sometimes even those who are not focused on their personal evolution experience higher states of consciousness. When this occurs, it is usually a life-changing moment. Such experiences are not random. I believe these are interventions from our souls for the purpose of getting our attention to their needs—to live a values-driven and purpose-driven life in our three-dimensional physical reality. The soul suddenly opens the doorway of our awareness to other potentialities, inviting us to grow and evolve. The defining characteristic of these higher states of consciousness is always the same: the absence of fear and a feeling of deep connection.

Transformation

The first realization I had from studying the states of consciousness described in Vedic philosophy was that the onset of soul consciousness corresponds closely to Maslow's need to "know and understand" and Carl Jung's concept of "individuation." This is the fourth level of consciousness. I called this level "*transformation.*" It is an essential precursor to self-actualization. Transformation is the level of consciousness where we begin to inquire into the true nature of who we are, independently of the culture and environment in which we were raised. At this level of consciousness, we are able to step back far enough from the cultural and social environment that has conditioned our beliefs to make our own choices so we can become the author of our own lives and develop our own voice.

The First Level of Self-Actualization

I believe cosmic consciousness corresponds to the first level of self-actualization. I refer to this level of consciousness as "*internal cohesion,*" the fifth of the seven levels of consciousness. At this level of consciousness, your ego and your soul blend together in unison. This is the meaning of internal cohesion. At this level of consciousness, you find your personal sense of transcendent purpose (soul's purpose). Your ego and soul become energetically aligned. You become a soul-infused personality wanting to lead a values-driven and purpose-driven life.

The Second Level of Self-actualization

I believe God consciousness corresponds to the second level of self-actualization. I refer to this level of consciousness as *"making a difference,"* the sixth of the seven levels of consciousness. At this level, you begin to uncover the deeper attributes of your soul. You develop a sense of knowing that goes beyond logic and reasoning, and your intuition plays a larger role in your decision-making. At this level of consciousness, you fully activate your soul's purpose by making a difference in the world. You quickly learn that the degree of difference you make can be significantly enhanced by your ability to collaborate with others who share the same values and a similar mission, vision or purpose.

The Third Level of Self-actualization

I believe unity consciousness corresponds to the third level of self-actualization. I refer to this level of consciousness as *"service,"* the seventh of the seven levels of consciousness. We arrive at this level of consciousness when the pursuit of making a difference becomes a way of life. When we reach this level, we become at ease with uncertainty and can tap into the deepest sources of wisdom. We learn to operate with humility and compassion.

Whilst I fully realize the correlations I have made between the Vedic philosophy and the Seven Levels of Consciousness may not be exact, they are sufficiently close to warrant our attention and provide insights into the motivations and underlying spiritual significance of the process of self-actualization.

Changing from needs to consciousness

The second change I made was to shift from needs to consciousness. It was evident to me that when people have underlying anxieties or fears about being able to meet their needs, their minds remain focused on finding ways to satisfy those needs. They are focused at the level of consciousness that represents the need they are experiencing.

Problems arise when the need is driven by a subconscious fear-based belief about being able to satisfy that need—what is known as an Early Maladaptive Schema. When this happens, you cannot get enough of what you think you need to assuage the subconscious fear, even though it would appear to an outside observer that you have satisfied that need.

For example, when a person has a fear-based belief at the survival level of consciousness, no matter how much money he or she earns they will always want more. For them enough is never enough. Such people can remain focused at the survival level of consciousness all their lives, even though they may have mastered some of their other needs—for example, they may be in a loving relationship and have all their needs met at that level.

Those who have underlying anxieties or subconscious fears about belonging or being loved subconsciously operate from the relationship level of consciousness. They have a strong need to experience affection or affiliation that was not accorded to them in their childhood. As adults they may compromise their own integrity to get these needs met. They want to be liked or they want to be loved. They find it hard to deal with conflicts and may use humour to reduce tensions and bring harmony to a situation. They are afraid of not being loved or accepted. They are dependent on others for the love they crave.

Those who have underlying anxieties or fears about their performance or ranking in relation to their peers subconsciously operate from the level of self-esteem consciousness. They have a strong need for recognition or acknowledgement that they failed to receive in their childhood. As adults the seek power, authority or status to get these needs met. They can never get enough praise or acknowledgement. Consequently, they become perfectionists, workaholics and overachievers. Despite all the accolades they may get, they are always left wanting more.

These considerations led me to recognize that our Early Maladaptive Schema (subconscious fear-based beliefs) directly influence the levels of consciousness we operate from and can block or undermine our ability to shift to the transformation (individuate) and internal cohesion (self-actualize) levels of consciousness. They show up in our lives as negative (potentially limiting) values such as greed, control, blame, status-seeking, etc.

> *Early Maladaptive Schemas (beliefs) seem to be the result of dysfunctional experiences with parents, siblings, and peers during the first few years of an individual's life. Most schemas (beliefs) are caused by on-going everyday noxious experiences with family members and peers that cumulatively strengthen the schema (belief). For example, a child who is constantly criticized when performance does not meet parental standards is prone to develop the incompetence/failure schema.*[1]

Re-labelling the lower levels of consciousness

The last change I made to Maslow's hierarchy of needs was to combine the physiological survival level and the safety level into a single category. I felt justified in doing this because it is our cells and organs (our body-mind) that regulate the physiological needs of our body, not our personal consciousness. Only in times of distress or dysfunction does our personal consciousness intervene in the functioning of the body. For example, our body sends signals to our personal consciousness when it needs food and water or needs to eliminate waste. Our personal consciousness is not in control of these natural functions. I named this combined level "survival consciousness" because it focusses on issues of physical survival, physical safety and physical health.

I also renamed the level of love/belonging: I gave it the name "relationship consciousness". I felt justified in doing this because our ability to experience a sense of belonging and love depends on the quality of our relationships. I did not rename the self-esteem level. The self-esteem level, together with the relationship level, represents our emotional needs.

I thus created three levels of human consciousness from the first four levels of Maslow's hierarchy of basic needs: survival consciousness (survival and safety combined), relationship consciousness (replacing love/belonging) and self-esteem consciousness. Together, these three levels of consciousness represent the emergence and development of the ego; the first three stages of psychological development.

With these three changes to Abraham Maslow's model (needs to consciousness, expanding self-actualization and relabeling the basic needs), I was able to construct a model of consciousness that corresponds to the evolution of the human ego and the activation of the human soul. Every level of the model represents an evolutionary need that is inherent in the human condition.

The needs we have generate motivations that in turn determine our behaviours. If you are unable to meet a particular need, your consciousness will keep returning to that level until you are able to satisfy that need. When we have learned to master the needs of a particular level, we automatically shift the focus of our consciousness and our motivations to satisfying our next most important need; usually a need that exists at the next higher level of consciousness.

Note

[1.] Jeffrey E. Young, *Cognitive Therapy for Personality Disorders: A schema-focused approach (revised edition)* (Sarasota: Professional Resource Press), 1994, p. 11.

ANNEX 2

World views and stages of psychological development

Table 6.1 (from *Evolutionary Coaching*[1]) which is based on the Spiral Dynamics model, shows a possible correlation between the stages of psychological development and world views. Let me stress that this mapping is approximate.

Table A2.1: Stages of psychological development and world views.

Stages of psychological development	World views
Serving	Holistic
Integrating	Integrative
Self-actualizing	People
Individuating	
Differentiating	Status
	Authority
	Power
Conforming	Tribal
Surviving	Survival

I would like to make the following comments on Table A2.1.

First, whereas it took three shifts of world views (power, authority and status) to gradually open up the possibility of the differentiation stage of psychological development to the masses, it took only one shift of world view (from status to people) to open up the possibility of the

77

masses experiencing the individuation and self-actualization stages of psychological development.

Second, whereas there are no societies operating with the integrative world view, some communities are beginning to experiment with this world view. This is something we can expect to see emerging in the communities of the most advanced democratic nations in the next few decades.

Third, the bonding that takes place in the tribal world view is different from the bonding that takes place in the people world view. Bonding in the tribal level world view is exclusive; it happens only in groups that share the same ethnicity or heritage. People of different ethnicities or with a different heritage are excluded from the group. Bonding in the people world view is inclusive; everyone in the same community and society, including people of different ethnicities is included as part of the group.

Fourth, viewed in its entirety, the framework of collective human emergence described earlier contains some evolutionary patterns. Each world view is progressively more inclusive: the criteria for community or society membership become less focussed on ethnicity and religion and more focussed on character or competence. Each world view progressively reduces the level of cultural fear and reflects a higher stage of psychological development and higher level of consciousness.

This finding is confirmed by my own research. In *Love, Fear and the Destiny of Nations*[2] I show that there is a strong link between the level of cultural fear in a nation and the level of democracy (as measured by the Economic Intelligence Unit's Democracy Index). As the level of democracy increases, the level of cultural fear decreases: and as fear decreases, the levels of equality and trust increase.

In *The Values-Driven Organization*[3] I show that the level of cultural entropy (impact of fear-based behaviours) reduces as organizations embrace the values associated with the higher stages of psychological development.

The shift in world views is now accelerating at a rapid pace. Whereas previously it took several millennia, then centuries, for new world views to appear, when the conditions are right (basic needs met and democracy established) new world views are now emerging in just a few decades.

The impact of this is that consciousness can evolve at a faster pace than ever before in human history because the barriers to psychological development have been removed. As more and more communities or societies are able to meet the basic needs of their people, more and more people in those communities or societies feel supported in moving from the differentiation stage of their psychological development to the individuation stage. This in turn creates pressures to implement democratic governance. Once democratic governance and principles are well established, people no longer experience the cultural fears that prevented them from individuating and self-actualizing.

Notes

1. Richard Barrett, *Evolutionary Coaching: A Values-Based Approach to Unleashing Human Potential* (London: Fulfilling Books), 2014.

2. Richard Barrett, *Love, Fear and the Destiny of Nations: The Impact of the Evolution of Human Consciousness on World Affairs*, (Bath: Fulfilling Books), 2012.

3. Richard Barrett, *The Values-Driven Organization: Unleashing Human Potential for Performance and Profit* (London: Routledge), 2013.

ANNEX 3

The Seven Stages of Psychological Development

The seven stages of psychological development occur in consecutive order over the full period of our lives. We begin the journey by learning to survive, and we complete the journey by learning to serve. Whereas the first three stages of psychological development are about developing the skills (physical and emotional) to master our deficiency needs, the last three stages are about learning to master our growth needs. Our ability to shift from focusing on our basic needs to focussing on our growth needs depends on many factors, the most important of which are as follows.

The level of psychological development of your parents

If the pressures to conform to the values, beliefs and traditions of your parents are strong, you may find it uncomfortable to explore your own values and beliefs. Your family may not understand why you want to be different or what you think is wrong with their way of being.

The level of cultural evolution of the community and society you are raised in

If the pressures to conform to the values and beliefs of the community and culture you belong to are strong, then you may risk censure, excommunication or even imprisonment if you begin the process of individuation. Your desire to have the freedom to explore your uniqueness will be viewed as a threat.

The level of education you attain

Unless you engage in some form of public or private education (or international travel) that is beyond the level attained by your parents, you may not be able to surpass their level of psychological development.

Your will power to explore your full human potential

It takes immense will power and courage to explore the higher stages of psychological development if the pressures to conform from your family, community and society are large. If you proceed, you risk cutting the bonds that enabled you to meet your basic needs. You risk isolation and loneliness.

For some or all of these reasons, the majority of people in the world never move beyond the third stage of psychological development. There is too much at stake (particularly for women and people living in authoritarian cultures) for them to risk exploring the higher stages of psychological development.

What holds people back is the fear of not being able to meet their deficiency needs and what pulls them forward is their search for meaning and significance.

The first three stages—surviving, conforming and differentiating—are stages of ego development that we all naturally pass through from the moment we are born up to the time we become young adults. How well we are able to master these stages of development—satisfy our basic needs and develop a healthy ego—will determine, to a significant extent, our ability to engage in the higher stages of development.

Whereas the first three stages of development are about learning how to survive in the parental and cultural framework of your existence where you are dependent on others to fulfil your basic needs, the fourth and subsequent stages of development are about discovering who you really are outside of your parental programming and cultural conditioning; embracing the unique sense of your own self and becoming truly independent, overcoming your dependence on those around you for your survival, relationship and self-esteem needs.

To fully embrace these higher stages of development, you must be prepared to let go of the aspects of your parental and cultural conditioning that you assimilated during the first three stages of your development that no longer serve you or do not align with who you really are. You must begin to embrace the values, beliefs and passions that you were born with that reflect your unique self.

Because of poverty, and the cultural and political circumstances in which the majority of people on the planet live, most people never get to the fourth stage of development. They live in a state of dependency, unable to individuate because they identify with the cultural and religious beliefs of their childhood and teenage years. Or, alternatively, they are held back from expressing their unique selves by repressive political regimes or strong religious cultures. It requires great courage in such circumstances to separate yourself from the crowd and become who you really are.

This is one of the major evolutionary benefits that modern economic and social development has brought about: by alleviating poverty and introducing democratic governance, we have enabled the masses to meet their basic needs and given them the freedom to individuate and pursue their growth needs.

If you are fortunate enough to live in a community or culture where uniqueness is celebrated, higher education is easily available, and you are encouraged from a young age to be independent (think for yourself) then you may begin to feel the pull of your soul towards the higher stages of psychological development—towards individuation and self-actualization—even during your early adult years.

In some rare cases, we find people—let us call them mystics—who attain the higher stages of psychological development without seemingly passing through the lower stages. They naturally evolve into soul consciousness without having experienced any significant ego needs.

The following text provides a brief description of the key features of each of the seven stages of psychological development.

Surviving

The quest for survival starts as soon as a human baby is born. At this stage, the infant is dependent on others to meet its physiological needs. The infant child instinctively knows, through its DNA programming, what it must do to establish itself as a viable entity in a physical world.

During this first stage of psychological development the child has to establish its own separate sense of identity, and learn how to exercise control over its environment so that it can get its survival needs met. If the child finds this task difficult, because its parents are not vigilant enough to its needs or the child is left alone or abandoned for long periods of time, the child's nascent ego will form subconscious fear-based beliefs (Early Maladaptive Schema) that the world is an unsafe place and that the people it depends on cannot be trusted.

If on the other hand, the child's parents are attentive to its needs, and are watchful and responsive for signs of distress, then the child will grow up with a sense of security and a belief that others can be trusted. Feeling physically safe and secure is the first and most important need of the ego-mind.

Conforming

The task for the child at this stage of development is to satisfy its need for love and belonging: It needs to feel safe in its familial framework of existence. The young child quickly learns that life is more pleasant and less threatening if it lives in harmony with its parents and siblings. Staying loyal to kin and community, adhering to rules, and participating in rituals and traditions are important because they consolidate the child's sense of belonging and enhance its sense of safety.

At this stage, the child subconsciously learns beliefs and behaviours that allow it to maximize its pleasure and minimize its pain. If punishment is used to assure conformity, then the child may adopt a strategy of blaming others to avoid reprimands. If the child believes the rules or reprimands are unjust or unfair, he or she may develop a rebellious streak.

If for any reason (poor parenting, lack of attention, etc.) the child grows up feeling unloved or doesn't belong, the child's ego may develop subconscious fear-based beliefs along the lines of the world is unfair, I am not important, or I am not lovable. Later on in life the child may find itself seeking affection, needing praise, and wanting fairness. The child will be on the lookout for friends, groups or communities where these needs can be met. Feeling safe, loved and a sense of belonging is the second most important need of the ego-mind.

Differentiating

During the next stage of psychological development, the differentiation stage, the child/teenager/young adult seeks to satisfy its need for respect and recognition. It wants to feel acknowledged and special—respected or recognized by parents, family, siblings, peers, teachers or gang members for excelling at something they can do well. The child/teenager/young adult wants to stand out from the crowd. The task at this stage is to hone your gifts and talents (the things you are good at) so you can develop a healthy sense of pride in your accomplishments and a feeling of self-worth. You want to feel good about who you are.

Your parents are instrumental at this stage of your development for giving you the positive feedback you need. If you fail to get this feedback, you will grow up with the subconscious fear-based belief that you are not good enough. You will feel driven to prove your self-worth. You may become highly competitive, attempting to seek power, authority or status so that you can be acknowledged by your peers or those in authority as someone who is important or someone to be feared. If your ego mind does not get the reinforcement that it needs, you could grow up with a feeling that no matter how hard you try, recognition escapes you—even when you are successful, it will never seem like enough; you will always be striving for more. Feeling a sense of self-worth or self-pride in your accomplishments is third most important need of the ego-mind.

If you were able to successfully transition through these first three stages of your psychological development without significant trauma and without developing too many subconscious fear-based beliefs about meeting your deficiency needs, then you will find it relatively easy to establish yourself as a viable adult in the cultural framework of your existence as long as you can find opportunities to earn a living that meet your survival needs.

Individuating

During the next stage of psychological development—the individuating stage—which under normal circumstances occurs between twenty and forty years of age, after we have experienced living the life of an adult, we will begin to feel the need to transcend our physical and emotional dependence on our family and the cultural groups we are embedded in by aligning with our own deeply held values—who we really are at the deepest level of our being.

The task we have before us at this stage of development is to embrace our freedom by separating ourselves from those aspects of our parental programming and cultural conditioning that no longer serve us, particularly the subconscious fear-based beliefs we learned in our childhood and teenage years about meeting our deficiency needs (early maladaptive schema) that keep us anchored in the first three levels of consciousness.

Learning to reduce the impact of your fear-based beliefs usually requires a lifetime of commitment to personal mastery. You will need to uncover, understand and release your subconscious fear-based beliefs about being able to satisfy your deficiency needs. Overcoming these ingrained patterns of behaviour will require you to build new neural pathways based on positive beliefs. By embracing your true sense of self, and living the values that resonate most deeply with how you are, you will establish your independence, build your integrity and start to seek your own path in the world.

Living the values that resonate most deeply with who you are means letting go of the decision-making modalities of the ego (beliefs) and embracing the decision-making modalities of the soul (values). The progress you make in this regard will dictate how well you are able to move through the self-actualizing stage of development. Living a values-driven life is an essential prerequisite for leading a purpose-driven life.

You will need to master the values and behaviours that build your integrity to be successful in living you're your passion. Individuating and leading a values-driven life corresponds to the first stage of soul activation.

There are billions of people on the planet who have difficulties individuating—they either live in conditions that make it hard for them to survive (earn a living), or they have sub-conscious fear-based beliefs they learned during childhood which keep them focused on seeking ways to satisfy their unmet physical and emotional needs. Individuating can be especially challenging if you live in a kinship or tribal culture, where people are dependent on each other for their survival, and where the pressures to conform are large.

If on the other hand, you grew up with self-actualized parents, who took care of your basic needs and treated you like a young adult, by teaching you to be responsible and accountable for your life and your emotions, then you will find it relatively easy to embark on the individuating stage of your development. Once you have learned how to master your deficiency needs, and have established yourself as viable and independent individual, you may feel a pull towards living a purpose-driven life.

Self-Actualizing

The self-actualization stage of development involves satisfying your need to find meaning and purpose in your life by uncovering your unique gifts and talents and making them available to the world. It also involves learning how to align your ego's motivations with your soul's motivations.

For most people, finding their soul's purpose, their calling or vocation, usually begins with a feeling of unease or boredom with the work they embarked on earlier in their lives, upon which they are now dependent for their livelihood. This can be a challenge, especially if the work that now interests you is less remunerative and less secure than the work you have been doing. Consequently, aligning with your soul purpose can bring you face to face with your survival fears.

You will know you have entered this stage of development if you no longer find it challenging. You may no longer have an appetite for what you have been doing. You will want to move from the work you thought of as a job or career, to focus on work that feels like your mission. As you begin to uncover your soul's purpose—the activities or work you are passionate about—you will feel new energies emerging.

Uncovering your soul's purpose will bring passion, creativity and vitality back into to your life. Your live will have meaning. Finding your soul's purpose and committing to it, represents the second stage of soul activation.

Integrating

The integrating stage of development involves satisfying your need to make a difference in the world by making use of the unique gifts and talents you uncovered at the self-actualizing stage. As you make progress in this endeavour you will begin to realize that the extent of the contribution you can make and your impact in the world is conditioned by your ability to connect and cooperate with others who share you values and purpose—people with whom you resonate and empathize. This is your soul community.

To make this shift from the self-actualizing stage to the integrating stage you will have to assume a larger sense of identity; move from being independent to being interdependent. Not everyone has the emotional capabilities to be able to make this shift. Integrating with others to make a difference in the world represents the third stage of soul activation.

Serving

The serving stage of psychological development involves satisfying your need to lead a life of service for the good of humanity and the planet by living out your purpose and thereby fulfilling your destiny. At this stage you begin to recognize the unity and interdependence of all things. This will affect your behaviours, your attitudes and every other aspect of your life. Making a difference becomes the central focus of your life.

You may find your workplace has become too small for you to fulfil your calling. You may need to find a new and larger role for yourself in society: you may become an elder in your community; you may become a mentor to those who are facing life's challenges; you may care for the sick or dying; or you may find ways to support young children or teenagers in dealing with the difficulties of growing up. Whatever you find yourself doing, it will in some way support the well-being of your community or the society in which you live. Deep down, you will begin to understand that we are all connected energetically, and that by serving others you are serving yourself. Selfless service represents the fourth level of soul activation.

The seven stages of psychological development occur in consecutive order over the full period of our lives. We begin the journey by learning to survive, and we complete the journey by learning to serve. We start our adult lives in ego consciousness; and if we are successful with our psychological development, we finish our adult live in soul consciousness.

You will find that as you move through these upper stages of development from self-actualizing to serving, you will need, from time to time, to dip back down to the transformation (fourth) level of consciousness to address and release deeper feelings of separation. In this respect, individuating/transforming is a never ending process: something you will need to focus on all your adult life.

For a more detailed account of the higher stages of psychological development, read *What My Soul Told Me: A Practical Guide to Soul Activation*.[1]

Note

[1] Richard Barrett, *What My Soul Told Me: A Practical Guide to Soul Activation* (London: Fulfilling Books), 2012.

INDEX